Challenging Power

ALSO AVAILABLE FROM BLOOMSBURY

Journalism in an Age of Terror: Covering and Uncovering the Secret State, John Lloyd

Modernity and the Political Fix, Andrew Gibson

Capitalism's Holocaust of Animals: A Non-Marxist Critique of Capital, Philosophy and Patriarchy, Katerina Kolozova

Right-Wing Culture in Contemporary Capitalism: Regression and Hope in a Time Without Future, Mathias Nilges

Ethics Under Capital: MacIntyre, Communication, and the Culture Wars, Jason Hannan

Challenging Power

Democracy and Accountability in a Fractured World

Cynthia Kaufman

BLOOMSBURY ACADEMIC
LONDON • NEW YORK • OXFORD • NEW DELHI • SYDNEY

BLOOMSBURY ACADEMIC
Bloomsbury Publishing Plc
50 Bedford Square, London, WC1B 3DP, UK
1385 Broadway, New York, NY 10018, USA

BLOOMSBURY, BLOOMSBURY ACADEMIC and the Diana logo are trademarks of
Bloomsbury Publishing Plc

First published in Great Britain 2020
Reprinted 2020

Copyright © Cynthia Kaufman, 2020

Cynthia Kaufman has asserted her right under the Copyright, Designs and
Patents Act, 1988, to be identified as Author of this work.

For legal purposes the Acknowledgments on p. viii constitute an extension
of this copyright page.

Cover design by Charlotte Daniels
Cover image: View of the collapsed Rana Plaza building from a nearby rooftop
(© Zuma Press Ltd / Alamy Stock Photo)

All rights reserved. No part of this publication may be reproduced or transmitted in any form or by any means, electronic or mechanical, including photocopying, recording, or any information storage or retrieval system, without prior permission in writing from the publishers.

Bloomsbury Publishing Plc does not have any control over, or responsibility for, any third-party websites referred to or in this book. All internet addresses given in this book were correct at the time of going to press. The author and publisher regret any inconvenience caused if addresses have changed or sites have ceased to exist, but can accept no responsibility for any such changes.

A catalogue record for this book is available from the British Library.

Library of Congress Cataloging-in-Publication Data
Names: Kaufman, Cynthia C., 1960- author.
Title: Challenging power: democracy and accountability in a fractured world /
Cynthia Kaufman.
Description: London ; New York : Bloomsbury Academic, [2020] | Includes bibliographical references and index. | Summary: "Arguing that we only have democracy when systems of power are held to account, Kaufman examines the real work being done to challenge the operations of power that underlie four unruly social problems: climate change, sweatshop labour, police abuse, and economic deprivation. In Accountability Democracy, Kaufman pairs each of these issues with an operation of power – the large scale influence of multinational corporations; the power of governments; the authority of financial markets; and the control inherent in systems of meaning – and using case studies like the Rana Plaza disaster in Bangladesh and the killing of Eric Garner, forcefully demonstrates the difficulty in challenging this nexus of power. Yet, advancing a positive message, Kaufman maintains that this network is not omnipotent and can be questioned if we develop 'mechanisms of accountability' which allow us to conceptualise the nature of these restrictions and the action required to resist them. Kaufman provides then, a model for ethical living that allows us to investigate and appreciate our own connection to the powerful forces that control our world"– Provided by publisher.
Identifiers: LCCN 2020009114 (print) | LCCN 2020009115 (ebook) | ISBN 9781350139053 (hardback) | ISBN 9781350139046 (paperback) | ISBN 9781350139060 (ebook) |
ISBN 9781350139077 (epub)
Subjects: LCSH: Power (Social sciences) | Government accountability. | Democracy.
Classification: LCC JC330 .K387 2020 (print) | LCC JC330 (ebook) | DDC 320.01/1–dc23
LC record available at https://lccn.loc.gov/2020009114
LC ebook record available at https://lccn.loc.gov/2020009115

ISBN: HB: 978-1-3501-3905-3
PB: 978-1-3501-3904-6
ePDF: 978-1-3501-3906-0
eBook: 978-1-3501-3907-7

Typeset by Deanta Global Publishing Services, Chennai, India
Printed and bound in Great Britain

To find out more about our authors and books visit www.bloomsbury.com and
sign up for our newsletters.

Dedicated to the memory of Rina Rehman, Berta Cáceres, and Eric Garner.

Contents

Acknowledgments viii
Preface ix

Introduction 1

1 States of Irresponsibility: Rana Plaza, Accountability, and Power 23

2 The Ethics of Accountability Democracy 35

3 Democracy in Crisis 59

4 Politics beyond the Polis, Democracy beyond Elections 73

5 The Destructive Powers That Need to be Held to Account 95

6 Accountability 127

7 Building Accountability Democracy 163

8 Acting Well in a Traumatized World 185

Notes 193
Bibliography 205
Index 211

Acknowledgments

Many friends and colleagues helped along the way with inspiration, detailed reading comments, suggestions for books to read, and encouragement. I would like to especially thank Joann Martin, Sunita Vatuk, Ricardo Blaug, Rebecca Gordon, Susanne Jonas, Michael S. Schudson, Katherine Sklar, Fred Block, Marian Mabel, Ron Hayduk, Derek Tenant, Raul Pacheco, Ishmael Tarik, Amy Merrill, and Dean Birkenkamp. I feel deep appreciation for the encouragement and quiet time given by my family, Rosa and Carlos Davidson. Finally, special thanks go to the team at Bloomsbury for being such a pleasure to work with, and to the anonymous reviewers who really helped bring what I was doing into focus.

Preface

I grew up with a deep sense of alienation. My two parents, my brother, and I moved a lot, and my parents were not social people. They tended to talk about what was wrong with the people around us, to keep to themselves, and to connect deeply only with our extended families, which were bi-coastal, and also on the move. My father's family is Jewish, and most of them have a sense of unease in the world, that is almost certainly related to the pogroms they fled at the turn of the last century. My mother grew up in ultrarich Greenwich Connecticut, at that time one of the wealthiest towns in the United States, in the mostly Irish community of people who worked as servants. My Irish immigrant grandmother was a nanny to the ultrarich. My Azorean grandfather painted the interiors of their houses.

I spent most of my formative years in San Diego in white middle-class suburbs. As I came into my teen years, I felt the world around me to be intolerably dull and devoid of any sense that anything mattered. I escaped two years early from my mostly white and middle-class high school because it felt like a prison. I mean that in a spiritual sense. It was not a high-security prison experienced by low-income people of color in the United States. But for a person like myself, curious to find what was engaging about life, it felt like it was crushing my soul. I made friends with kids from around our region who were artists and intellectuals. What we shared was a sense that the world of suburbia that we were headed to inherit was frighteningly without meaning.

In 1980, during my wandering drop-out years, I encountered an article about the war that was then raging in El Salvador. A revolutionary movement was working to overthrow a brutal dictatorship, and the US government was on the side of the dictatorship. I was deeply moved by a sense that I was connected to those atrocities, and that if I joined with others, I might be able to make a difference. I reached out to the Committee in Solidarity with the People of El Salvador—an organization mentioned in the article—and got swept up into the movement to stop US support for the war and to support the revolution. It was the first time in my life that I felt like I was part of something worth throwing my passion into.

When I think about my relationship to the political struggles that have defined my life since that moment, I am struck by how connected I feel to the world of social justice. How do people feel connected to the troubles of the world and what is the nature of those relationships? How and why do people in the Global North care about the people who were crushed to death in Rana Plaza in Bangladesh in 2013? How do we see our connections to the distant processes that cause so much fossil fuel to be burned that our planet is on track soon to be inhospitable for human society? How do we understand our relationships to the mass and social media cultures which put commercial interests in between our connections to the world and each other, and which help create our own sense of self and meaning? How do we understand our relationships to those dominant systems of meaning which dehumanize so many types of people, which lead to people being murdered by police, who act in the interests of a state over which we have little control?

How do we disembodied and unembedded wandering Jews (and by that I don't just mean people of Jewish heritage, but most people who have grown up in the interconnected, but also fragmented, and highly mediated world of global society) understand our connections to the world we are trying to make better?

If democracy is about challenging relations of power, and if power is constructed, deployed, and also to be constrained, through large-scale often global social processes, how do we understand the nature of what binds us to the movements that are working to hold power to account? What is the nature of our connections to distant others and how does, or can, that drive our engagements in the world? Are the emotional connections that pull me to that work based on an abstract disconnected set of principles which should be resisted? Or is it the task of those of us living in this world of thin, fragmented, and unrooted connections, precisely to find our sense of purpose in those ephemeral webs through which we are connected?

I don't know the answer to those questions and don't intend to answer them in this book. But I do know that, for whatever reason, many people find themselves troubled by their connections to the horrors that constitute our present world. Our lives are woven together through networks of anonymous relationships constructed by markets, through transnational media, through intertwined political systems. As I write this, I am connected to them through my inability to breathe comfortably, as climate change–created wildfires make the air in almost all of Northern California, where I live, dangerous to breathe. For many of us, that thinly connected network of relations is the only world we know.

Each of us, in our own particular ways, is faced with the question of how to live a good life in a world where power is increasingly concentrated and not held to account, and increasingly destroying the very fabric of our human and ecological existence. We each feel that pain in different ways, and we each struggle for ourselves to make sense of the ways we are implicated in problems over which no one seems to be responsible, which we all have some limited abilities to impact, but where there are no clear lines of responsibility.

This book attempts to understand the nature of our own individual places in holding power to account in a political world of myriad connections which are thin, not grounded in stable senses of place, history, or community, and which often feel empty and disassociated. It is dedicated to the search for ways to make these hard-to-grasp connections as understandable as possible, in order to clarify the moral and political tasks before each of us, as we find ways to live together that make life worth living and keep the planet habitable.

Introduction

It breaks my heart, but there really isn't anything I can do about it. I mean who am I? I'm just one person, and if I got involved in trying to change all that, I would just end up turning myself into a social outcast and not accomplishing anything.[1]

But it is your fault. You are the ones who are privileged by the whole system. The system allows you to live in comfort and luxury. And don't act so innocent. You know perfectly well what is going on. And you know perfectly well how to stop it. I want you to remember every time you fill your gas tank that what is flowing from that hose is the blood of my people.

How can companies spend millions to sow confusion about reality and get away with it and still be considered respectable parts of society? Can't anyone just take responsibility? Can't we hold those companies responsible and just stop them? Why is everyone so apathetic? Makes me crazy.

You people don't even know how good you have it. If everyone were to just take responsibility for their own lives and take care of business it would all be fine. I'm not responsible for someone who dies in some country on the other side of the world. Sure, I feel sorry for them, who doesn't? But are we supposed to bleed ourselves dry saving them from themselves?

You all can just keep on fighting, because I am just trying to get by in this world. I do what I need to do to survive. Don't get me wrong. It hurts me that there's so much pain in the world. But the people who are making the mess need to be the ones to clean it up.

...

How do we live well in a world where we are deeply connected through complex social processes to terrible things that are happening, but which we don't control? What do we do about the fact that those complex processes often lead to people and other living beings suffering tremendously from things that are not their fault? How do we go about our business happily when the atmosphere that supports all living beings is in serious peril? Who do we hold to account for cultures so toxic that they survive in ways that kill people?

We are living in a period in which many people feel guilty, powerless, frightened, and frustrated. What is it about the way our society is organized that makes it seem like no one is responsible for anything, while simultaneously seeming like we are all a little bit guilty of everything? What is it that makes many people want to find someone to blame, yet unable to figure out whom to hold responsible, and for what? Are there ways to have a better understanding about our own responsibilities, such that we can live with clearer consciences? Are there ways to help build political and social systems that actually work to keep terrible things from happening?

How can we gain a better understanding of those complex social processes that connect us, but also slip from our grip when we try to hold anyone responsible or try to change those systems to make them more just? Are there limitations in the moral and political concepts we use that make them not up to the task of helping us live well and find our places as actors in our world which is increasingly connected through markets, social media, and transnational processes, but also fragmented by the ways those connections uproot people from deeper, more sustaining and empowering connections? Are there concepts we can use to hold the powerful accountable, and to orient us to our places in the reality of an increasingly interconnected, frighteningly fragmented, and deeply unjust world?

One purpose of this book is to help those who are troubled by these questions to get past a sense of paralysis that many have when facing them. It is intended to offer tools for moving toward a deeper understanding of the nature of our interconnections, so that we can have a better sense of our roles in the things that happen, and of what we can and should do about them. The other purpose is to help us understand the large-scale and increasingly interconnected systems of economy, politics, government, culture, and society in which we are embedded, so that we can advocate for changes that will lead to those systems being more able to serve our needs to live well together. By better understanding the nature of the systems of domination that we face, we can then better understand productive ways of dealing with them.

A theory of morality that will help us understand how to hold power to account must deal with a broader and more diffuse set of actions than moral philosophy generally does. The conceptual tools used in Western philosophy are best at holding us responsible for the intentional actions we take with respect to individuals who are close to us in space and in time. An approach to politics that will help us develop systems that hold the real powers we face to account will need to focus on more than the workings of governments. It will need to focus on more than setting up legal and regulatory frameworks limited to actions that take place within a national territory and that cross a line of infringing on others.

We are at a time of a crisis in accountability. In our interdependent, networked world, there is a devastating weakness in the systems that exist to hold power to account. The world is full of ways that people's lives, and the very air we breathe, are destroyed at an alarming rate. And yet so many of the things that are causing that destruction are not the job of anyone, or any institution in particular, to stop.

The crisis of accountability is an outgrowth of the expansion of capitalist processes ever further into our global systems. An important part of pro-capitalist thinking is the idea that major social decisions should be left to markets which will allocate social goods without the need for coordination, with no one being responsible for how they operate. One result of the past several hundred years of expansion of the capitalist aspects of our societies is that the world is now dominated by huge transnational corporations, whose power transcends the ability of governments to control them. It is also dominated by transnational institutions which operate in the interests of capital. And governments are in many ways captured by those who seek profits, at the expense of human and environmental needs. Our social systems and systems of meaning are deeply distorted by our lack of grounded connection in communities, and by the ways that we are connected through systems of media and consumer culture that are run for profit.

To develop the tools we need to stop the kinds of horrors this book addresses and increase our ability to hold power to account, we need to look at ways power is configured, such that it is not easy to control or even perceive. The configurations of power that are causing the crisis in accountability are large, such as transnational corporations; slippery, such as the workings of the market; contested, such as the power in states that claim to be neutral arbiters of conflict and controlled by all of us; and elusive, such as the workings of systems of meaning. Accountability is a critical tool that can be used to orient our actions in challenging these unruly configurations of power. To hold power to account requires that we make it visible, inquire into how it operates, draw attention to illegitimate operations of power, and stop their replication.

At first sight it may seem strange to focus on accountability. There are many ways that the right wing uses the rhetoric of accountability to support unjust operations of power. We are told that social welfare systems need more accountability mechanisms, so that taxpayer resources are not wasted. Yet the systems' setup to catch cheaters often cost more than cheating ever did. Generally, these right wing calls for accountability are actually not motivated by a real sense that there is waste or fraud in a system. Instead, they are often cynical attempts to undermine support for the provision of social services or protection of rights.

In 2018, the US state of North Dakota decided that only people with a street address would be able to vote. Those pursuing this policy knew full well that there was not real problem of people without street addresses voting fraudulently. Instead, this was a brazen attempt by Republicans to disenfranchise Native Americans, who disproportionality vote Democrat, many of whom live on reservations which don't use street addresses.

In both of these examples, a rhetoric of accountability is used to further an illegitimate operation of power. For that reason, I call these cynical attempts pseudo-accountability. Sincere attempts to make a system more efficient, or cost effective, or honest, can come from people with any political perspective, including the right. But sincere attempts at accountability are something different from the dominant right wing attempts to use a rhetoric of accountability to build their power.

Perhaps because of its cynical overuse by the right wing, but even more, for very particular self-imposed reasons, accountability has not been a particularly strong concept on the left. When talking about unjust operations of power, people on the left tend to focus on oppression and domination. They suppose that when systems of oppression or domination are undermined, society is fine. Leftists tend to talk a lot about power and about the ways that capitalism, and other systems of domination, such as racism and sexism, oppress us. They work to free society from domination. But by focusing on the quest for freedom from oppression, there is something important that we leftists often miss. We tend to not focus much on how to create social systems that prevent unjust forms of power from accumulating. That attention to the negative questions, of challenging the bad, often happens at the expense of attention to ways of building the good which are resistant to abuse.

The great theorist of capitalism, Karl Marx, believed that once class society was abolished, there would be no reason for people to systematically mistreat one another. And so, his work has surprisingly little to say about how to develop accountable social and political structures. The lack of a theory of accountability in Marx, and in the Marxist tradition, has had disastrous consequences. In numerous instances, pro-capitalist states were overthrown and replaced with a "dictatorship of the proletariat," which did not fade away and turn to true egalitarian communism, as predicted. Rather they persisted as dictatorial regimes. Missing from Marx's critique of capitalism was an affirmative theory of how to hold to account the forms of power that proliferate in a state. A just society requires more than the election of people who hold good values. It also requires there to be systems in place to hold those people accountable to the people who elected them, and which will check their ability to misuse their power.

Anarchists argue that holding state power is always a bad idea. For them, governments are by their nature oppressive systems of domination. Even more than Marxists, Anarchists tend to focus their political critiques on the social processes that limit human freedom. Anarchist thinkers have provided important correctives to the ways Marxists focus on simply taking state power and overthrowing the bourgeoisie. They have a lot of helpful things to say about the oppressive nature of the state and capitalist economic processes. But they have even less to say than Marxists about how to create large-scale systems of social interaction that are resistant to the accumulation of power.

Accountability has become an increasingly popular concept among liberals, especially those doing transnational work to reduce poverty or improve the environment. Increasingly, projects working in these fields are developing systems of feedback mechanisms where projects are to be held to account to global funders or the communities they are intended to impact. Often missing in these liberal accountability regimes is a broad understanding of the operations of power in which these accountability regimes operate. Typically, problems are addressed, without looking at the large-scale systems that create those problems in the first place. Instead accountability is reduced to a set of mechanisms to inspect individual projects.

This book takes a broader frame, and looks at how a wide variety of operations of power can be held to account. It uses the concept of accountability to theorize how illegitimate operations of power can be challenged. By putting those operations of power at the center of the analysis, it avoids the narrow frame of much liberal work on accountability. By focusing on the needs to develop robust systems to tame and manage power in an ongoing way, it attempts to fill in a void in much left-wing thinking. And by taking seriously an analysis of real operations of power, it avoids the empty rhetoric of many right-wing calls for accountability.

The worldwide crisis in accountability can be addressed by taking seriously how power operates in the current social world, developing an understanding of what the effective ways are to hold power to account, and getting clear about what each of our roles are in making that happen. When mechanisms to promote accountability proliferate, they can be seen as creating accountability democracy.

Accountability democracy is a framework for understanding the actions people take to challenge unjust operations of power. Accountability mechanisms are mobilized by people all the time to challenge systems of domination. This is not a call to a different way of acting to build a better world. Rather, it is a framework for understanding better what we are doing when we are working for social justice. And it is a call for paying more attention to ways to hold power to account.

Work to hold power to account, and limit how it flows, can be understood as made up of accountability mechanisms. Effective accountability mechanisms have five parts: voice, values, responsibility, sanction, and power. We take actions that give *voice* to pains and conceptualize those pains as violating normative social *values*, we name actors who should be held *responsible* for those pains, we engage in work to *sanction* those responsible, and we work to add *power* to make those sanctions have impact. Accountability democracy is made up of actions taken to strengthen accountability mechanisms.

This book focuses on four ways that power gets channeled, concentrated, and deployed into configurations of power, each of which needs to be understood to face current the crisis in accountability, capitalist markets, governmental sovereignty, transnational processes, and systems of meaning. These four configurations of power are not meant to be exhaustive.[2] Taken together they are intended to illuminate, in broad brush strokes, the underlying causes of some of the major problems we face.

Each of the four configurations of power is tied with an example that will be used throughout the book to illuminate how that problem appears to our everyday consciousness, how it operates at a deeper level, and how it can be held to account. The examples are not meant to be exhaustive of the problems caused by that operation of power. The example of police violence is used to explore the nature of elusive configurations of power. Much of what is said about the underlying causes of elusive configurations of power can also be used to understand the roots of gender-based forms of domination. And each of the real problems the book looks at has elements of each of the configurations of power operating in it. But each will be looked at mainly through the lens of one, so as to help illuminate that particular configuration of power. Each example is also used to show how the concepts of accountability mechanisms and accountability democracy can help clarify what is at stake in the real fights people are engaged in to hold that configuration of power to account. The examples are meant to be illustrative.

Rana Plaza and the Power Hidden in Markets

The questions raised about who to hold responsible for the collapse of Rana Plaza in Bangladesh in 2013 illustrate the accountability challenges manifested in the ways that power comes to be concentrated, and hidden from moral scrutiny, in markets. The decision of the left-wing Syriza government in Greece—to accept an onerous financial deal offered by European bankers—tells us important things about the challenges of holding large-scale transnational operations of power to account. When we look at attempts in the United States to deal with climate change, we can see important things about the nature of governmental sovereignty and how governments are places where power is concentrated, deployed, and contested. Finally, the murder of Eric Garner by Daniel Pantaleo of the New York Police Department (NYPD) raises troubling questions about the ways that discourses of dehumanization enable violence to be perpetrated against some of us, without the limitations that apply to things done to those whose full humanity is recognized.

The concept of accountability democracy will be shown to help us understand the nature of the real-world work being done to challenge each of the configurations of power behind each of these illustrative examples. Organizers working on these problems are challenging power in a variety of ways, and the concept of accountability mechanism can help clarify how those challenges to power work, and what is needed for them to be as effective as possible.

In 2013, when the Rana Plaza building, which housed small factories cranking out clothing for the transnational market, collapsed in Dhaka, Bangladesh, people all around the world wondered whom to blame for the disaster. As the media were beginning to unravel what went wrong, it became clear that the webs of blame stretched from Sohel Rana, the owner of the building, to a variety of building inspectors, to the ruling party in Bangladesh, to the promoters of free trade deals. The blame also stretched in uncomfortable ways to anyone in the world who buys clothes.

The collapse of Rana Plaza raises questions about the nature of global capitalist markets and the ways that people come to be implicated in the lives of others through a chain of highly anonymous interactions, which leave no one seemingly responsible for terrible things that are a regular part of our lives. There is a form of agency that gets constituted by "the market" that comes to be seen as an autonomous entity having its own needs, and which functions in ways that undermine attempts to limit the power of capital to destroy lives. Markets are a slippery configuration of power.

We develop accountability democracy when we reduce the slipperiness of markets by calling out the intentional decisions which shape them, when we fight against trade deals that shape markets in the interests of transnational capital, and when the workers in Bangladesh collaborate with transnational actors to pressure companies to increase building safety. Just as we are all in some ways implicated in these disastrous configurations of power, so are we also all capable of participating in a variety of ways in strengthening the accountability mechanisms that hold these configurations of power to account.

The Greek Economic Crisis and Transnational Systems of Power

The situation faced by the people of Greece in 2015 can help us to look at another aspect of global capitalism—the role of large-scale actors, such as transnational finance institutions, in causing problems that are too large for governments to easily control. In 2015, the Greek people were suffering under the weight of loans that had been taken on by a corrupt government. The people then elected the Syriza-led government that was expected to say "no" to the transnational financiers who were insisting that those loans be repaid in ways that would be devastating for the Greek people. Shortly after that vote, the government tried to negotiate better terms for those loans, failed at that, and then agreed to accept a bailout which has led to the extreme immiseration of many Greek people.

This situation exposes configurations of power that are so large that mechanisms for holding them to account are underdeveloped. The Greek government was faced with an almost impossible choice between defaulting on the loans, and possibly crashing the economy, on the one hand, and capitulating to the European institutions on the other. There is much disagreement about whether or not the Syriza government made the right choice when it capitulated, and yet it is clear that at the moment of the crisis there was no good option.

One of the most important aspects of an accountability mechanism is that a problem is seen as caused by some sets of actors, who are then pressured to change the situation. Accountability democracy does not ask who has been authorized to take action to solve a problem, who the agents are, or whose job it is to solve it. Rather, it analyzes the landscape of a problem and asks what the leverage points are that can be impacted to hold power to account. In this case, an increase in accountability democracy would mean that there was a functioning accountability mechanism that could have forced the transnational institutions destroying Greece to change course. And those of us outside of Greece would do well to focus on what could be done to pressure those institutions, more than on what the Greek government should have done in a very difficult situation.

The Climate Crisis and Power in Governments

Many important things are being done everywhere in the world to deal with climate change. Governments are enacting policies to reduce emissions. Organizations are pushing for those changes. Clean energy is now economically competitive. Individuals are reducing their carbon footprints. Millions of people, organizations, and institutions all around the world are acting to make a difference in large and small ways.[3]

And yet most of us feel overwhelmed by the magnitude and urgency of the climate crisis, and by how many aspects of our social fabric need to be changed, rapidly, to prevent the worst outcomes. Governments can enact rules that prevent the burning of fossil fuels, and they can incentivize the development of clean forms of energy, energy saving, and good product and regional design. But in the United States, the forces pushing for those changes are up against an industry that holds trillions of dollars in assets it stands to lose if we make those changes and which has spent at least a billion dollars trying to influence public opinion and to capture and control governments to thwart action on climate change.[4]

That situation helps us to see how governments act as vectors for power, preventing some accumulation of power, while enabling others. It raises the question of the nature of rule of law and how governments operate to concentrate power, to make certain flows of power normalized and accepted, while also regulating and limiting other flows of power.

People in many countries feel increasingly powerless to have an impact on the ways their governments operate. People all around the world are beginning to see notions of electoral democracy as empty promises to influence states that are not able to deliver the good lives they hope for, while being run by and in the interests of elites. Governments are an example of a configuration of power that is in its nature contested.

It is important to not see government as a neutral result of democratic processes. Rather, the real powers that are operating in any given governmental structure, whether it be a nominally authoritarian government or a nominally democratic one, need to be faced and challenged with the development of accountability mechanisms. In the case of the US government and climate change, accountability mechanisms need to be developed that expose the impact of money on governmental decisions; find ways to strengthen the responsiveness of government to the interests of the people; and be clear about which aspects of the problem can and should be solved by government, and what other avenues exist for significant change.

Police Violence and the Power In Systems of Meaning

Mass incarceration and police violence are another area where many people feel a sense that the problems we face are intangible, the lines of responsibility blurry, and the solutions beyond reach. Many of us in the United States are horrified by the ways that the police can murder people of color with impunity. The murder of Eric Garner by Daniel Pantaleo of the NYPD raises questions about how the very humanity of whole groups of people (in this case, Blacks in the United States, but in many other instances, religious and ethnic minorities, women, queer people, or people with disabilities) are socially constructed in ways that deny their full humanity. This construction then leads to the idea that they are not deserving of the moral and legal deference that limits the use of violence against those whose full humanity is seen.[5] Police murder is one example of the ways that operations of power are enacted through elusive systems of meaning, in this case, the meaning of who is seen in their full humanity.

Holding those powers to account involves the development of all five aspects of an accountability mechanism. On the spot videos of some high-profile cases have given *voice* to the pain of communities which have lost someone to police violence. The hashtag #BlackLivesMatter has put what had been seen as routine police operations into the *values* framework that shows the reality of Black Lives not mattering to the criminal justice system to be an urgent social problem. The Movement for Black Lives is working to hold specific city governments responsible for the actions of the police they are accountable to supervise. They are running people for office, pressuring office holders, and pursuing lawsuits, to mobilize the *power* needed to change practices. Those mobilizations of power are in some cases leading to *sanctions* on police departments to prevent future acts of police murder.

The book begins with an introduction to these ideas of accountability democracy, accountability mechanisms, and the powers that need to be held to account in Chapter 1. Chapter 2 looks at ways that each of us can be said to be accountable for challenging the complex powers we face. It explores the nature of our ethical responsibilities in the face of problems that are embedded in complex and diffuse configurations of power. It also explores how the moral burden of the problems of the world can be understood in ways that help us see our responsibilities to act, but which do not lay those responsibilities on us so heavily that they lead to inaction.

Chapter 3 then goes on to explore the present global crisis of democracy. Chapter 4 stretches the ideas of politics, democracy, and citizenship, to help us understand the nature of accountability democracy. Chapter 5 analyzes the nature of the large-scale, contested, slippery, and elusive configurations of power we face, which need to be held to account. The core of the book is in Chapter 6 which develops in detail the concept of accountability and explores how accountability mechanisms work.

Chapter 7 gives a detailed exploration of how each of the problems, and aspects of power, analyzed in the book, is at present being challenged by current work being done to develop accountability mechanisms, and how we understand the roles in these solutions for people who have different relationships to the problems. Finally, Chapter 8 brings the issues explored in the book back to the personal level and offers a set of suggestions for how best to move forward as a person, with an understanding of our world as deeply interconnected, shot through with relations of power, impacting everyone and transformable by all of us.

We are living in a time of a crisis of accountability in part because we are living at the bleeding edge of a five hundred year expansion of pro-capitalist and consumerist ways of understanding our relations to one another; of communities being fragmented by capitalist processes; of discourses of dehumanization being proliferated in order to make whole classes of people easy to exploit for profit; of the impact on our political and social systems of unlimited concentrations of wealth in the hands of a few individuals and corporations.

Accountability is an important issue for our times, in part, because of the ways that pro-capitalist ways of thinking make it disappear. One of the ethical claims made by those supporting capitalism is that we are each responsible mainly for ourselves. Government is supposed to set up a framework of law to keep people from interfering with one another. People are encouraged to not see the systems of power that connect us, and to not see themselves as agents able to transform those systems.

This is a result of the conceptual frameworks that underlie pro-capitalist ways of understanding the world. The market is supposed to take care of the economy. I buy what I buy based on what product suits me best. Pro-capitalist ways of thinking don't ask me to wonder who made it or its impacts on the climate. Manufacturers outsource jobs to stay competitive. Subcontractors pay low wages to stay in business.

In a society that is dominated by pro-capitalist ways of thinking, Adam Smith's "invisible hand of the market" is understood to be responsible for the ways many elements of our social dance are coordinated. The human decisions that shape those markets, the powers that keep market relations functioning, and the individual choices that people make over the ways they participate in markets, are all made largely invisible by the myth that markets function on their own to make social choices natural and inevitable.[6] With pro-capitalist ways of thinking, we end up with a situation where everyone is responding to conditions for which no one is asked to take responsibility. And so, it works as a mechanism for undermining accountability.

Forms of domination embedded in our very notions of humanity, and of whose humanity matters, constitute the systems of meaning that we inhabit such that the needs and interests of some people are met by social systems, while those same systems normalize violence and deprivation for others. There are ways that those systems of meaning make these forms of deprivation seem normal and natural, and allow them to be reproduced without anyone being held to account for them.

Other problems are constituted by the way that governments function as sites of contestation. Any government will have a set of rules and practices, which enable some forms of interaction and disallow and punish others. Who is well served and who is poorly served by those systems or rules are the results of fights over power that take place over generations. Legal systems have embedded in them the history of past struggles. States come to have rules of law that come to be normalized and which concentrate power and allow it to flow in some ways and block its ability to flow in other ways. If we want to hold power to account, we need to deal with the power concentrated in states.

Understanding the nature of the powers we face is a prerequisite to understanding the tasks before us for building a better world. Equally important is understanding, in practical terms, how to hold those powers to account, and how to stop them from proliferating. For the past few hundred years many thinkers have posited that the spread of representative democracy was the most crucial step in challenging power. And yet it is becoming increasingly clear that representative democracy is not up to the job of constraining the four configurations of power investigated here.

Representative democracy is not a sufficient tool for challenging the slippery power of markets and for challenging the power of transnational corporations which operate beyond the bounds of a national territory. Nor is it up to the task of holding to account systems of meaning which incite violence and deprivation against people seen in ways that negate their full humanity. And while representative democracy is the tool used to make governments accountable to their people, if we want to challenge the powers that constitute our present moment, the ways that power comes to be embedded in representative democracies, in very uneven ways, also needs to be questioned.

Accountability democracy is meant to be a broader concept than representative democracy. Representative democracy understands the *demos*—or the people—as constituted by individuals living in a particular territory. It supposes the issues to be deliberated on by the *demos* to be those having to do with systems of law anchored in government. In contrast, accountability democracy asks us to work at all levels of social reality to challenge a wide variety of damaging operations of power, wherever they are found.

Representative democracy anchors challenges to power in the processes of elections, constitutions, and the rule of law. Accountability democracy anchors challenges to power in the broader framework of the use of accountability mechanisms. Elections, constitutions, and the rule of law can be seen as three different accountability mechanisms, among many others.

An accountability mechanism is traditionally seen as having two aspects: voice and sanction. The voice side of accountability asks us to expose injustices. The sanction side asks for consequences, such as punishment. The theory of accountability mechanisms developed here expands those crucial aspects of accountability to include three more elements: *values* that give meaning to the thing being voiced as a legitimate problem; a clear line of *responsibility* to address the sanction to someone in particular; and finally, the *power* to make the sanction have impact. The voice needs to have meaning, the sanction needs to have a target, and the sanction needs to be enforceable.

The accountability mechanisms that need to be developed in order to have a robust accountability democracy require more subtle attention to the workings of accountability mechanisms than standard theories of accountability offer. The devastating powers that need to be reined in are often not seen as social problems in need of social solutions; are not seen as the fault of anyone in particular; and often require novel forms of counterpower to hold them to account.

Because of the ways that pro-capitalist ways of thinking make it such that no one is seen as responsible for many of the terrible things that happen in the world, it leads to social patterns in which the bonds that connect us become invisible. Nominally, democratic states seem neutral on their surface, become another place where power is made invisible, and so where it becomes unaccountable. Systems of meaning too have ways of mobilizing resources, and to use the example of racism in the United States, of leading to some people thrown in prison because of the fears and hatreds of others.

Developing systems of accountability under such circumstances requires that we work to make those invisible systems visible, and that we find ways to park responsibility for changing those systems at certain people's doorsteps as their obligation to change. We need moral concepts that are up to the task of helping us to see who, and what, are responsible for the wrongs that happen in the world.

Typically, the sanction side of accountability asks us to pressure those responsible for doing wrong, so that they do not do wrong in the future. A narrow view of that sanctioning focuses on punishment. And yet, who do we punish for the pressures of the market? A view of sanction that is focused on punishment is not nearly robust enough for the present circumstances. Thus, we need to rethink the sanctions side of accountability to be something more akin to a restorative approach, which focuses on how to keep wrongs from happening, and which involves creating systems of consequences to disrupt the social patterns that cause harm.

Accountability democracy involves the proliferation of these five-parted accountability mechanisms, wherever unaccountable power is found. By exploring the nature of some of the significant configurations of power we face, offering a framework for understanding the ways we challenge those configurations of power, and investigating where each of us sits at the crossroads of power and accountability, this book is intended to clarify the tasks facing those who want to live moral lives, and act in effective ways to build a better world.

We need mechanisms of accountability that will work in the slippery world dominated by capitalist processes, where the mere act of shopping for clothing at the lowest price is part of a chain of connections that leads to buildings falling on people and killing them; where simply going about our daily lives and doing what other people expect of us is leading us to destroy the atmosphere; where governments can follow routine sets of rules, and those rules lead to some people's lives being devastated; where some people voting in ways that seem right to them, leads to others going to prison and having their lives destroyed.

We need mechanisms of accountability that will keep governments from being able to mobilize violence that destroys people's lives based on the fears that politicians can activate within our systems of meaning. And we need mechanisms of accountability that hold small-scale actions, such as the burning of fossil fuels as a regular part of our lives, to account. This book looks at ways to understand moral and political responsibility that are relevant to our deeply connected and fragmented world, where we are all acting and acted upon by many social systems, material processes, systems of meaning, and networks of relations.

As an author, and a committed activist, I am concerned with helping to motivate and clarify our common work toward building a world where power is held to account. To help you as a reader connect with this rather abstract set of issues, each chapter starts with fictional voices based on expressions of how people located in different places in society might experience those questions, try to answer them, and try to avoid them. I invite you to feel your way into the text, and observe how the ideas in it mix with your own commitments, ambivalences, and evasions.

The text tries to offer pathways beyond feelings of guilt, powerlessness, and fear. It points to ways we can clothe ourselves without buildings falling on people and killing them; ways we can go about our daily lives without destroying the climate; ways we can enjoy the pleasures our cultures offer us without that leading to others having their lives devastated; ways to set up rules under which we can live well together without that leading to anyone having dictatorial power over us; and ways to have a sense of which actions we should take to repair our very broken world.

1

States of Irresponsibility
Rana Plaza, Accountability, and Power

When I shop, I do wonder who made the things I am buying. It takes so much of the pleasure out of it. But I really do think about it. Today I looked in my closet and none of it spoke to me. It all felt a bit drab, so I went to the mall. There I saw all sorts of beautiful things. When I tried them on, I felt much fresher. I bought a few shirts and a nice new purse to go with them. I wore the shirt out to dinner with a few friends and one of them said "Cute top!" I didn't tell that friend that when I got home from the store, I had looked at the tag and it said "Made in Bangladesh." I thought about the story I had read the day before about Rina Rehman, who died in the building collapse. I didn't tell them that I sat on the bed and felt sick. What was I doing? Could Rina Rehman have made that shirt? I didn't tell them, because I didn't want to ruin the fun everyone was having, and I was embarrassed about being the one who always ruined people's fun. And I am certainly not going to stop Rana Plazas from happening by not buying clothes or by becoming a social outcast.[1]

No amount of dithering will take away the reality that you are, in the end, responsible for the people crushed to death in global factories. They were hired to make your clothes. And they died doing so.

Punish the companies that are destroying the environment; punish the politicians who sow hate; punish the greedy bastards who own sweatshops. Pretty simple really.

Well punishment, that makes sense to me....no one ever gets dinged for the stupid things they do. Don't blame "the system." But, if someone does something wrong, of course they should be punished. Throw the bastards in jail who broke the law. But I'd rather not hear about it. Those people don't know how to run their countries. And no amount of bellyaching from you will make them stop treating each other like that.

As long as you blame the ones who are causing the problem, and leave me, and my clothes, and my car out of it, I wish you well. It's easy for you to get all moralistic about what people wear. I am just trying to get by in this world. I buy cheap fashion because it's what I can afford. And I need to look good for work. So, I hope all of you who have the time to worry about those things figure out a way to feel good about your clothes. In the meantime, I'm buying the best I can for the cheapest I can.

The language of "it's all about supply and demand" covers the reality that we live in a world of human relations mediated by systems of power and privilege.

...

On April 24, 2013, the Rana Plaza garment factory collapsed in Dhaka, Bangladesh. Those accounting for the deaths have said that 1,129 people died, and 2,500 people were taken from the building alive.[2] The world was horrified by the human tragedy, and simultaneously thrown into a state of introspection about who to hold to account. A sickening feeling took hold among many who feel that we are all in some sense a part of the web of relationships that caused this tragedy to happen. The tendrils of blame spread far and wide and reached all parts of the globe, leaving people in many parts of the world feeling impotent and frustrated.

...

"Lutfer Rahman, whose wife, Rina, worked at Rana Plaza, was sipping tea in their damp one-room home when a neighbor yelled through his doorway: The plaza was gone. Lutfer and Rina had married in their hard-bitten farming village and, like legions of people, moved to Dhaka for better prospects. They soon had two daughters, Arifa and Latifa, and Lutfer had supported the family by pulling a rickshaw until asthma forced him to quit. So, Rina had become the breadwinner, a factory helper passing materials to sewing operators for 5,000 taka ($62) a month. Now, for the first time since he'd given up his rickshaw, Lutfer ran: about half a mile through the winding labyrinth of dirt lanes and workshops, past blacksmiths and brick kilns, trailed by his daughters. They reached the site just as two bodies were pulled from the wreckage, neither of them Rina's. Lutfer, overwhelmed by the rising din of sirens and shouting, bent over to catch his breath...

On May 10, after viewing well over 500 corpses, twelve-year-old Arifa Rahman found her mother. Her body was badly damaged; Arifa may have passed her by several times. But the newly added name on the body-bag tag read: Rina Rahman, husband: Lutfer Rahman, district: Rangpur, taken from a stained document... removed from a pocket. The family's search had ended. It also secured them a 200,000-taka ($2,500) *check from an ad hoc relief fund administered by the prime minister. They received another 20,000 taka for burial costs.*

The Rahmans loaded Rina onto a rickshaw bed and headed home. In the family compound, relatives washed the body and cloaked it in a cotton shroud. That same day, Rina was buried in a small graveyard near their house. The land is overgrown and no headstone marks her plot, but Lutfer knows the place."[3]

...

If we look at who is responsible for the deaths caused by the Rana Plaza building collapse, at one peel of the onion we see the managers who had forced the employees back into the building, even after the workers had refused to enter because they had seen cracks in the building the previous day. But, of course, those managers were just doing their duty to their bosses, the factory owners. The owners were merely fulfilling the orders they had from the multinational corporations. The corporations were working to keep up with the pressures of the market.

It is easy to focus on Sohel Rana himself. Rana and his parents had engaged in bribery and illegal maneuvers to obtain the land that the factory was built on from small-scale land owners. When the disaster happened, Rana tried to flee the scene and was caught a few days later at the border with India. Initially, he was granted bail, but after protest from labor organizations, he was held in jail, where, as of this writing, he remains awaiting trial in five different cases. His mother, Morzina Begum, also ended up in jail.

Other standouts for blame were the building inspectors who approved a building constructed on a pond covered with sand, and who allowed Rana to add three floors of industrial production to a building that was designed to be residential.[4] The chain of causality doesn't stop there with the most egregious violations of law. Government ministers refused UN aid in the rescue effort because it might have hurt national pride. This left many people to die who would have been rescued alive in a well-run operation.

When they were ordered to go back into the building, even though they knew it was unsafe, most workers chose to go back because they were threatened with losing a month's salary. A strong union would have provided a structure for collective resistance to that threat and probably would have saved people's lives. There are unions in Bangladesh, but the environment for them is not very hospitable. Companies routinely hire thugs to beat and sometimes murder labor organizers.

Both major Bangladeshi parties are run by people who benefit from low-wage manufacturing. Corruption is endemic to the political system. There are many causes for that, having to do with ethnic rivalry, the ugly legacy of British colonialism, and the legacies of the Cold War.

And, of course, capitalism is an important part of this picture, and that's the part that connects those of us outside of Bangladesh most strongly to this tragic story. This story is about more than an unfortunate thing that happened because of local corruption in a small and poor country.

The simple law of supply and demand says that people will buy more if the prices are lower, and companies will naturally look to where the prices are lowest. As unions fought and succeeded in moving the US garment industry past the sweatshop phase, companies raced to the bottom, and kept moving around the globe until they found places with the best environment for the cheapest production. Bangladesh is just a current holder of the honor of being a great deal for those looking for a cheap supply of labor.

Are the shoppers who buy cheap fashion to blame for playing the game of supply and demand? One of the most powerful aspects of pro-capitalist thinking is that we are encouraged to not ask that question. Consumers are supposed to look for the deals that suit them the best.

The questions then become: How do we hold ourselves and others accountable for the real operations of power that exist in this world? How do those operations of power create systems that are destructive? And how do we challenge the complex systems of power that we face?

Accountability

> accountable: Liable to be called to account; responsible (to persons, for things).
>
> account: Counting Reckoning, calculation, statement of moneys goods or services, Calculate compute, reckoning, and answer for.[5]

A system of accountability, or an accountability mechanism, works to hold agents to account for something that goes wrong. It does not necessarily involve punishment, but it does involve identifying those responsible for a problem in the hopes of preventing future problems.

If someone lets me down, and I don't let them know, they are likely to do that thing again. If I give them feedback and let them know that a something bad happened, then there is more of a chance of the thing not happening again. If my child always leaves her dishes on the table and I don't say anything about it, she is likely to keep doing it. I don't need to punish her to get her to clear her dishes, but there needs to be some form of feedback from her action to my reaction, for me to get a different action. There are many forms of feedback, and many reasons that people do things that are negative to others. Accountability mechanisms create forms of feedback from the negative things that happen to ways to prevent those actions from happening in the future.

Theorists of accountability focus on ways to create mechanisms that make the negative impacts of an action become part of the decision-making process about whether or not that thing will happen again. A productive accountability mechanism creates cycles to constantly monitor, constrain, and limit the way social processes operate.[6]

One of the biggest problems with pro-capitalist ways of thinking is that they undermine these systems of feedback. One of the basic premises of pro-capitalist thinking is that people with resources should be able to do what they like with their resources, and the role of government is to interfere as little as possible to allow individuals to make those choices. The networks of relations which create a social fabric, that holds us all in complex relations with one another, become invisible. And the presumption becomes that we are not responsible for one another. Rather, each of us is merely responsible for doing what's best for ourselves, limited by the requirement that we stay within the law, and we respect one another's individual rights. Morally accountable social relations are undermined by claims that we are all free and independent and have no obligations to one another.

Accountability for the Rana Plaza Disaster

We can and should rely on traditional notions of morality and responsibility to blame Sohel Rana for his part in the Rana Plaza disaster. As a moral agent he had all kinds of power to make choices other than the ones he made. According to Kantian philosophy, we are supposed to treat all people as ends in themselves, worthy of human dignity. On this criterion Rana failed. He treated the workers as means to his ends of self-enrichment. On utilitarian grounds we can say he acted immorally because more unhappiness came out of his managers telling people to go back into the building than if they had not. And of course, our old-fashioned legal concepts also work: if anyone deserves to be in jail, Sohel Rana does. The building inspectors who accepted his bribes can also be sent to jail.

Those are helpful steps, but they are not enough to prevent disasters like this from happening in the future. Most of our thinking about accountability has its roots in legal thinking, where laws are supposed to protect the common good, and those who break the laws are held accountable through punishment, such as fines or jail time. Our legal systems were created to constrain the acts of individuals, and they are generally best when applied to actions taken with intent to do wrong.

Retributive justice, the dominant approach to law, where individuals or corporate entities are punished for wrong doing, can be used in many productive ways to constrain the destructive powers we face. But retributive justice needs to be supplemented to get at problems which don't hit the high thresholds of responsibility required to trigger legal action. To develop effective ways to constrain the abuses we face, we also need to include ways to capture the social in our understanding; we need to be able to attend to the ways that we are all interconnected; we need to find ways to work prospectively to create accountability mechanisms that prevent harm. We need to supplement retributive justice with ways to heal the world to get at the roots of the problems we face. The linkages between my action of buying a shirt and the deaths at Rana Plaza are too weak to provoke traditional retributive forms of accountability.

In *The Imperative of Responsibility: In Search of an Ethics for the Technological Age*, Hans Jonas argued that in earlier periods of human history, the time and space horizons of our actions were much more limited than they are now. The move to more connected ways of living has led to the rise of new circumstances, and the ethical systems we have inherited are not designed to deal with them.

> The good and evil about which an action had to care lay close to the act, either in the praxis itself or in its immediate reach, and were not matters for remote planning. The proximity of ends pertained to time as well as space. The effective range of action was small, the time span of foresight, goal-setting, and accountability was short, control of circumstances limited. Proper conduct had its immediate criteria and almost immediate consummation. . . . Ethics was accordingly of the here and now, of occasions as they arise between men [sic] of the recurrent, typical situations of private and public life. The good man was the one who met these contingencies with virtue and wisdom, cultivating these powers in himself, and for the rest resigning himself to the unknown.[7]

Societies that are based on face-to-face interactions tend to have accountability mechanisms, where the consequences of actions are seen and where the society as a whole can make adjustments and come up with better rules, based on social needs. To answer the questions we are dealing with here, we need an ethical philosophy that asks how we act well in a world of increasingly distant interconnections and where the consequences of our actions lie far from the small group of people we know well.

If a small self-sufficient community is using farming practices that deplete its soil, people will notice that, and it will matter to them, and they will be in a position to shift their farming methods to maintain the health of their soil. One of the problems with the dispersed social networks that we currently inhabit is that those systems of feedback between a problem and a solution, and between a problem and a sense of who should deal with it, are broken. That leads to a weakness in accountability mechanisms to regulate our systems for the social good.

To build concepts of accountability that will help us navigate the present crisis of accountability, we will need to do more to bring the background network of social relations, or the social fabric, into view as part of conversations about morality and justice. We will need to connect the moral with the political. And we will need to focus on ways to foster accountability democracy where we have robust mechanisms to monitor and challenge the destructive configurations of power that cause harm.

Pro-capitalist ways of thinking have developed exquisitely to undermine accountability mechanisms. Consumers are only responsible for buying what pleases them. Manufacturers are only responsible for making a profit. Governments are only responsible for creating and enforcing laws that set the framework in which business can prosper, and which people respect each other's basic right to be left alone. Racism, sexism, and other systems of domination are woven into the social fabric, such that harms happen in ways that seem like the normal routine way that things are supposed to operate. In contemporary cosmopolitan culture, our responsibility is to enjoy. Each of us playing our role leaves huge gaps in responsibility that allow the climate to be destroyed, buildings to fall, a culture of consumerism as a path to status, and masses of people to be incarcerated.

Many people deal with their connections to the fabric of harm that is embedded in our social world by denying their connections to the larger social fabric we inhabit. Shrinking one's moral universe to those close in space and time to ourselves is one strategy for fending off a sense of malaise that comes from seeing those connections, but not doing anything about them. Others live with their hearts open to the world of interconnection and feel thrown into what can be an immobilizing sense of guilt and shame. Still others are motivated to act by that sense of connection to an infinite number of pains, and work themselves into misery trying to attain a sense of moral goodness through their social activism.

Having a clearer sense of what our responsibilities are in the face of these problems, and a clearer understanding of the ways to discharge those responsibilities, can help us live with our sense of the world open to the fullness of the realities we live, while at the same time living good lives.

2
The Ethics of Accountability Democracy

I treat people well. And I have a lot of empathy. It breaks my heart when I hear about people without enough to eat, or when a not so huge earthquake in Turkey kills thousands because the building standards are so low. I didn't make those things happen. And I have no power over the people who did. It makes me sad, but who am I? I can keep treating people well, be kind to those around me, and take responsibility for my actions. Maybe if everyone did that it would spread. So maybe the world becomes better from each of our own personal models of good behavior. Isn't society just the sum total of each of our own individual actions? [1]

But you are thoroughly guilty. Shell Oil stole our land, made it uninhabitable, and massacred those who resisted. They did that for your gasoline. If you aren't guilty, then who is? And it is your stupidity and complacency that allows Shell Oil to do what they do. You allow the politicians to get away with protecting and abetting Shell Oil. And might I remind you that you people get to elect the masters of the world who allow Shell Oil to

destroy our land and murder our activists? Moral people act and take responsibility for the things they make go wrong. You are part of the system that made this all go wrong. Therefore, it is your responsibility to do something to change the situation. And please don't tell me you are too busy. Do you have any idea how hard people work in my part of the world?

Morality is huge for me. Everything I do is for my family, and honor is king. A person who doesn't follow through on their commitments is scum. I follow the Ten Commandments, and that does a pretty good job telling me what to do. I'm pretty sure if everyone did that, we wouldn't have the messes we have. But it burns me up when people tell me to feel sorry for people who do nothing to take care of business and improve their lives. I do not make them steal from each other.

Morality asks you to think about the world as an individual and asking what you can do while still saying in your bubble of comfort, and without disrupting the devastation caused by capitalism. You don't exist as an individual. You exist as a part of the matrix. And if you are going to survive you are going to need to make that matrix healthy and sustainable. And for that you are going to need a team. And that team is going to need to do things that you weren't taught were the things you were supposed to do. I don't think morality is even the right thing to look at. The problem is caused by power, and so politics is what is needed to solve it. Morality tells you to think like an individual. Not very helpful here.

Whenever I think about all that is wrong in the world, it makes me feel guilty. And that sometimes makes me feel kind of resentful. I mean, it really isn't my fault. Well maybe it kind of is too. But I don't see how my feeling bad about it is going to make anybody's life any better either. When activists start complaining about how bad it all is, I want to tell them to stop. I know all that, or at least if I don't know all the details, I know the general idea. But what do you want me to do about it? I didn't make all that happen, and I do have my own life to live.

My morality is based on the word of God. All the problems I see break my heart. And I hope that by living a righteous life and following the path of the gospel, I can leave this world more blessed than I found it. I treat people well. I do what I can and donate to help feed the people who are hungry. I hope that means I am living a moral life.

. . .

For 500 years, as an economy built on plunder and slavery has evolved, along with it have evolved moral philosophies to justify slavery and plunder. Bentham says: "Nature has placed mankind under the governance of two sovereign masters, pain and pleasure. It is for them alone to point out what we ought to do, as well as to determine what we shall do." For 500 years, people in the West have been encouraged by their philosophers to pursue their individual happiness, with no accountability to anyone. Over the course of those 500 years, people's sense that they owe anything to anybody as fellow human beings has been thoroughly corroded. They feel alone and powerless. And nothing they are taught in school helps them understand their predicament.

. . .

Once upon a time a group of people found themselves in a state of nature, with property but with no connections to one another. Each one was an adult man, and each one was independent. Those independent men used their reason and reflected and found that the voice of reason, which is the voice of God told them that

> The state of Nature has a law of Nature to govern it, which obliges every one, and reason, which is that law, teaches all mankind who will but consult it, that being all equal and independent, no one ought to harm another in his life, health, liberty or possessions; for men being all the workmanship of one omnipotent and infinitely wise Maker; all the servants of one sovereign Master, sent into the world by His order and about His business; they are His property, whose workmanship they are made to last during His, not one another's pleasure.[2]

And those independent people of God had property and they used it productively, and they respected each other's property. And they bought and sold freely. And no one told anyone else what to do. And they were free and they had liberty.

But on that day when the state of nature began, other people, who had no property, also inhabited that state of nature. And the people without property said, "we'd like to buy and sell freely too, but we have nothing to sell." And the ones with property said, "you too can buy and sell freely because we are all free and all have equal rights. Freedom applies to everyone. You do have something; you have your ability to labor. Sell me your ability to labor and I will trade that for some food. And the price we set for those things will be based on how much you want to sell your labor and how much I want to sell my food. And we will both be free and we will both be independent, and we will both be under the law of the God called reason. And that free choice will be called liberty."

And those free independent people who were rational and independent and who owed nothing to anyone, and who were free and had property, sailed halfway around the world and found that there were people there who didn't live in a state of nature, but who had bonds and connections and shared their land and used it according to rules that were thousands of years old. And the free ones said, "Reason which is my God, tells me that land must be used in the most rational way and you are not doing that, and so that land by right of reason belongs to me."

And so, they took the land from the ones who lived according to rules and bonds that were thousands of years old.

> God gave the world to men in common; but since he gave it to them for their benefit, and the greatest conveniences of life they were capable to draw from it, it cannot be supposed he meant it should always remain common and uncultivated. He gave it to the use of the industrious and rational. ³

They found that those people who lived according to rules and bonds that were thousands of years old did not use the reason that free people used and they decided that those people could not be trusted to follow the reasonable ways of the timeless obligation-free world. And so, they enslaved them. For, if I see that someone does not follow the God called reason, that person could suddenly turn on me, and so that person has no rights,

> for the same reason that he may kill a wolf or a lion; because such men are not under the ties of the common law of reason, have no other rule but that of force and violence, and so may be treated as a beast of prey, those dangerous and noxious creatures, that will be sure to destroy him whenever he falls into their power. ⁴

In this world all that mattered were the present and reason, and decisions that were made to buy and sell and trade and make agreements.

And those reasonable people who had reason for a God lived happily ever after. Until one day the unreasonable people who lived according to *bonds and rules that were thousands of years old pointed out to them that the atmosphere had become toxic.*

...

"There Is No Such Thing as Society"

In his *Two Treatises of Government*, seventeenth-century British philosopher, John Locke, asked us to begin our thinking about politics by imagining that we were all born into a state of nature in which no one has any connections to anyone else. He then asks, what are the minimal kinds of agreements people would need to have between them to make that situation be functional? Those agreed-upon connections, such as property contracts and a minimal government, are the only social connections that they are asked to attend to. All other social connections are imagined away. By grounding his philosophy in that thought experiment, Locke encourages a way of thinking that makes our real, lived connections with one another hard to conceptualize. This way of thinking is at the root of the current crisis in accountability.

Conservative philosophy follows strongly in this tradition and talks a lot about responsibility and accountability, but that almost always means personal responsibility, as in: each person needs to take responsibility for themselves and the circumstances of their lives. Conservatives tend to believe that too much government makes us dependent and not responsible for ourselves. They argue that as people come to take responsibility for their own lives, they live better.

Ronald Reagan once said,

> We must reject the idea that every time a law is broken society is guilty rather than the law breaker. It is time to restore the American precept that each individual is accountable for his actions.[5]

And Margaret Thatcher famously said, "There is no such thing as society." In Reagan and Thatcher's world, we are each responsible for our own actions and for what happens in our lives. This philosophy is not very helpful for understanding the complex social processes that do bind us and create what the rest of us call "society."

This general focus on the individual as the main unit of analysis is fundamental in Western moral philosophy as well. In his introduction to Karl Jaspers's *The Question of German Guilt*, Joseph W. Koterski, writes that Western moral philosophies generally "attend to a person's intention in isolation from the embodied nature of any action or from the wide-reaching consequences of personal choices."[6]

Dealing with the questions of how to live well as moral people in a world full of unaccountable and destructive powers requires that we bring society to the foreground, and that we think across the silos in which morals and politics are generally kept. Moral philosophy typically asks the question, "What is the individual responsible for to be a good person?" Politics, on the other hand, is supposed to ask the question "what makes for a good government?"

In Plato's *Republic* the word for both moral goodness and political goodness is the same: *dikaiosyne*. It means something like righteousness. Some translators translate it as justice and others as morality. For Plato it meant both. For Aristotle the question of what it means to be a good person was deeply wrapped up in the question of what it means to have a good society. He believed that you could not fully be a good person without living in a good society.

Many African philosophical traditions begin with the assumption that the individual and the community are co-creating, and so ethical and political systems are interrelated. Bringing harmony to a society is linked with good action for the individual. And building a good society is seen as crucial for an individual to live well.

According to the South African Philosopher, Michael Onyebuchi Eze, "The 'I am' is not a rigid subject, but a dynamic self-constitution dependent on this *otherness* creation of relation and distance."[7] According to the Nigerian Philosopher Segun Gbadegesin,

> There need not be any tension between individuality and community since it is possible for an individual to freely give up his/her own perceived interest for the survival of the community. But in giving up one's interest thus, one is also sure that the community will not disown one and that one's well-being will be its concern. It is a life of give and take. The idea of individual rights, based on a conception of individuals as atoms, is therefore bound to be foreign to this system. For the community is founded on notions of an intrinsic and enduring relationship among its members.[8]

Beginning in the Enlightenment, ethical thinkers in the European tradition began to see morals and politics as two separate questions. This period gave rise to the ethical subject as an individual wondering about how to be good in a world taken as an unproblematic background. In his *Grounding for the Metaphysics of Morals*, published in 1785, Immanuel Kant argued that a moral person would follow the categorical imperative: to act as if one's actions were based on a rule that would be universal for all people.[9] Like Locke's state of nature, the categorical imperative is something that any person can access by reflection. It is grounded in common sense and the reasoning of the thoughtful individual.

Following the categorical imperative leads a person to not steal because a world in which everyone stole would not be a good world, and to not murder, based on the same reasoning. Kant's moral philosophy has been foundational in how people think of ethics in the West. And, in contrast with the approach taken by Plato, Aristotle,

Eze, and Gbadegesin, it is based on seeing a person as autonomous and outside of a network of fraught social relations.

Shortly after writing the *Grounding for the Metaphysics of Morals*, Kant wrote a response to criticism that had been raised about his work. In "On a Supposed Right to Lie because of Philanthropic Concerns," Kant discusses the example of a person whose friend is hiding in his house from a murderer. Kant had asked whether or not it is right to lie when the murderer knocks at the door. Kant argues that it is wrong to lie even in this case, because it is inherently wrong to lie.

Kant scholar, Helga Varden, defends Kant's position by imagining that the murder at the door is a Nazi. Varden argues that Kant's political philosophy says that a civil society is one that includes basic principles of justice. Varden claims that Kant has two sets of rules for action, one public and one private. In private interpersonal relationships, it is never right to lie. On a public level, it is right to follow the laws of a just society. And we have no obligations at all to a tyrannical government. Varden argues that heroes who committed acts of violence in opposition to the Nazis suffered later in life because they knew that while their violent acts against Nazis were right in a political sense, they were wrong in a moral sense, having violated the categorical imperative.[10]

Kant's categorical imperative gives us universal rules for how a moral person should act regardless of the circumstances, and as Varden argues, if we live under tyranny, the circumstances may force us into immoral action. If we don't live under tyranny, then we should always act according to the categorical imperative. Kant's philosophy, like that of Locke, and of Enlightenment philosophy more generally, presumes a good society in which morality is about the rules for making private choices.

That presumption of a good society may have held for the narrow circle of life Kant saw himself as a part of in the small, orderly town of Königsberg, where he spent his whole life. But the Enlightenment movement that Kant helped develop was also part of a set of larger projects. The Enlightenment period of European history is often credited with bringing the world democracy, science, and reason. But it was also the period that saw the birth of slavery and colonialism. Until fairly recently, the negative realities of slavery and colonialism were generally seen as unfortunate side stories of an overwhelmingly positive set of ideas bequeathed to us by the Enlightenment.

One early blow to that way of understanding the Enlightenment came from Martinican poet and philosopher Aimé Césaire. In his 1950 essay, *Discourse on Colonialism*, he made a powerful claim that from the beginning "European Civilization" contained a deep brutality.

> What, fundamentally, is colonization? To agree on what it is not: neither evangelization, nor a philanthropic enterprise, nor a desire to push back the frontiers of ignorance, disease, and tyranny, nor a project undertaken for the greater glory of God, nor an attempt to extend the rule of law. To admit once for all, without flinching at the consequences, that the decisive actors here are the adventurer and the pirate, the wholesale grocer and the ship owner, the gold digger and the merchant, appetite and force, and behind them, the baleful projected shadow of a form of civilization which, at a certain point in its history, finds itself obliged, for internal reasons, to extend to a world scale the competition of its antagonistic economies.[11]

For Césaire, humanistic values such as "the rule of law" were always to be seen as related to the brutality he sees as fundamental to the "antagonistic economies" capitalism. Underlying the period of colonialism and slavery was a society based on an economics of profit. Much important intellectual work—to help make sense of that reality and facilitate its development—was done by the leading thinkers of the Enlightenment period. They reconceptualized human beings as sovereign private individuals, responsible to follow rules but not responsible for the fabric of their social relations. This period's much valued focus on the rights of the individual was profoundly wrapped up with the idea that individuals have few obligations to one another or for the network of social relations they inhabit. As long as the Kantian moral subject was good, by virtue of his not lying to the man at the door, what happened to the victim hiding in the house was not his moral responsibility.

Government, or the public realm, was also reconceptualized during the Enlightenment to meet the needs of expanding capitalist processes. Government was seen, especially by Locke, as a night watchman state. Its job was to ensure that sovereign individuals didn't violate each other's spheres of privacy, and that the contracts that were the basis of capitalist markets would be honored.

The dominant moral philosophy of this period tends to shrink the scope of the ethical subject to a concern with private matters, and to suppose that the network of relations that hold us together is part of another set of concerns outside the realm of ethics. Increasingly, politics becomes the art of creating the structures that would allow sovereign individuals to pursue their private interests unimpeded by others, and allow interactions to be mediated to the extent possible by the anonymous forces of markets.

In order to deal with the power relations that we face in the present time, we need moral theories that are not based on this tradition of the separated private individual. Our moral philosophies need to focus on the ways that we are interconnected, and invite us to attend to better to ways to live well together in the world as we find it, fragmented, and built upon connections that cause harm. We need political philosophies that help us to see operations of power that are broader than the forms of power in government. We need to develop political systems that interrupt those operations of power and hold the powerful accountable. And we need moral and political concepts that help us to understand our responsibilities for co-creating the world that is made and transformed by our actions.

Morality and Social Connection

Accountability requires that we see the connections that exist between people, that we understand ourselves as living in a world where our relations with one another matter, where we all share some responsibility to better the health of the web in which we live. If we lived in a society with strong mechanisms of accountability, then there would be means by which we could connect specific actions to the consequences that harm people and the environment. We would then all be held responsible for maintaining the health of those systems of accountability.

In her essay "Responsibility and Global Justice: A Social Connection Model," Iris Marion Young takes up this problem, and asks how we can understand our moral responsibilities for people to whom we are only loosely connected.[12] She focuses on sweatshops as a central case for investigating the nature of responsibility. She looks at the responsibilities held by different people in the chain of affairs that connect us all to the wrongs suffered by people at the hard end of that chain of connections. She creates moral concepts to help us understand the interconnected realities we live.

Young argues that standard concepts of morality tend to look at situations in which blameworthy action can be pinned on an individual, where the action was done with intent, and where there is intent to do wrong. Western legal systems are built upon this notion of moral wrong, and the idea that some kinds of moral wrong are so serious that the government must punish them.

Young shows that this individualistic and quasi-legalistic sense of morality doesn't capture the sense that many of us have that we are somehow connected to the terrible things that happen to others. Young asks us to attend to the webs of connection in which we are embedded. She claims that we are responsible for the processes we are a part of enacting. The responsibility we have is not necessarily a legal liability for those actions and their consequences. But, if we want to be moral, we need to see ourselves as connected, and that means that our sense of ourselves as doing good, or of being blameworthy, is connected to the social processes we help enact.

> Finding an agent responsible does not imply finding the agent at fault or liable for past wrong, but rather refers to agents' carrying out activities in a morally appropriate way and aiming for certain outcomes. What I propose as a social connection model of responsibility draws more on the latter usage of the term "responsibility" than on the liability usage. It does share with the liability usage, however, a reference to the causes of wrongs—here in the form of structural processes that produce injustice. The social connection model of responsibility says that individuals bear responsibility for structural injustice because they contribute by their actions to the processes that produce unjust outcomes.[13]

She lays out the five main features of social connection model: (1) it does not isolate a few who are responsible; (2) it takes background conditions seriously; (3) it looks forward more than it looks backward; (4) the point is not to blame or punish or seek redress, but to enjoin those who participate to change systems; (5) and finally, responsibility is discharged by the actions we take as part of collective processes.[14]

And, she argues that not all who have some responsibility share the same responsibility. She worries that someone could read what she says as an argument that we are all equally to blame for sweatshops, since we are all connected to them in some way through the fabric of our shared lives. In response, Young writes, "The power to influence the processes that produce unjust outcomes is an important factor that distinguishes degrees of responsibility."[15]

She claims that we can understand responsibility through the lens of four parameters: power, privilege, interest, and collective ability. With regard to power she argues that our responsibility is relative to the power we have to make a difference. "An agent's position within structural processes usually carries with it a specific degree of potential or actual power or influence over the processes that produce the outcomes."[16]

In terms of privilege:

> Middle-class clothing consumers in the developed world, for example stand in a privileged position in the structures of the apparel industry.... Persons who benefit relatively from structural injustices have special moral responsibilities to contribute to organized efforts to correct them, not because they are to blame, but because they are able to adapt to changed circumstances without suffering serous deprivation.[17]

She argues that it is important that those wanting to challenge a system of injustice take seriously the perspectives of those most hurt by it.

> Those who are victims of structural injustice often have a greater interest in structural transformation.... Victims of injustice have the greatest interest in its elimination, and often have unique insights into its social source and the probable effects of proposals for change.[18]

Finally, she encourages us to think about which actions to choose to act on based upon our collective ability to make a difference. "Sometimes a coincidence of interest, power, and existing organization enables people to act collectively to influence processes more easily regarding one issue of justice than another."[19] Decisions about how we can be most effective are important for choosing where to act. We can understand ourselves as moral agents fulfilling our responsibilities to the extent that we engage thoughtfully and purposefully with a mind to making a real difference in solving the problems to which we are connected.

Morality in the Face of Power

To take the forms of action required to be a moral person in Young's sense often requires that we go against the grain of society as it is currently structured. It calls upon us to reweave the patterns that make up our social fabric. Contrary to some notions of morality that encourage us to not make waves and to keep our heads low, if we follow the implications of Young's view, being moral often means going against social expectations.

Our individualistic society asks us to think of our actions as if there was no social fabric and as if each interpersonal interaction were an autonomous act, and our morality lay in each of those individual choices. This leads people to want to take actions, such as boycotting certain companies, and purchasing from ethical companies. These actions can be positive, but they are not enough to transform the social fabric.

We solve our systemic problems together and by taking social action. To be an ethical person is to be a person who acts responsibly to heal the harmful patterns that exist in the world. Being moral in a connected world is not just about following the Ten Commandments, or the categorical imperative, and avoiding hurting people. It requires us to attend to the myriad ways we are interconnected, and to act as we can to improve the fabric of those connections.

Responsibility without Shame

When figuring out what to do with Young's idea that we are all interconnected, it is important to understand the relationship between guilt and responsibility and what it means to have a moral obligation. If my clothing purchases were part of a chain of action that led to Rana Plaza collapsing and killing Rina Rahman and more than a thousand other people, what does that imply for me? Young claims that we have a moral responsibility to act, and she wants to encourage positive action based on that sense of responsibility. She says we have a moral duty to attend to the social processes that we are part of enacting.

When we start to think this way, it is easy to feel overwhelmed and guilty. When we feel guilty, we are very likely to retreat into our privacy and narrower notions of morality in order to protect our ability to feel good about ourselves. And yet the happiness that comes from walling ourselves off to the ways that we are connected is a hard one to maintain, since it cuts us off from connection to the social fabric that is our shared reality. It can lead to its own unhappiness as many people who live their lives this way end up with a deep sense of disconnection and purposelessness.

Being responsible actors in a deeply distressed social fabric can have its own pleasures, as we find meaning and a sense of purpose in that work, as we are able to open our eyes and look at the whole of our social reality without flinching, and as we see ourselves as part of a team of millions working to heal the world. None of us can take on all of the changes that a person is capable of making. But each of us can be part of the large team that is engaged in that work.

When Young says we all have responsibility, that does not imply that we are bad people if we don't work ourselves to death doing all we can to challenge power. Her approach does not have hard edges that tell us where our duty begins and where it ends. This work leaves a fundamental ambiguity about how much, and what, a person is morally obligated to do.

Guilt

Often conversations about responsibility are short-circuited by a sense that looking at our interconnections will lead to feelings of guilt. In his essay "White Man's Guilt" James Baldwin talks about the ways that fear of feeling guilty often pushes white Americans to not see the realities of racism. The fear that they will be seen as guilty leads them to minimize the realities of racism and the ways that they are connected to the historical processes that continue to lead to racist outcomes.

> This is the place in which it seems to me most white Americans find themselves. Impaled. They are dimly, or vividly, aware that the history they have fed themselves is mainly a lie, but they do not know how to release themselves from it, and they suffer enormously from the resulting personal incoherence.[20]

White Americans often feel that when they look honestly at their history, their only option is to feel guilty and since they don't want to feel guilt and don't believe themselves to have done anything wrong, their only option is to avoid discussions of race. And when racial discussions are forced upon them, they are likely to feel confusion, discomfort, guilt, and resentment.

Because of this, guilt is often paired with its twin, denial. Fear of feeling guilty helps people keep their eyes closed. When I first got involved in social justice work, I focused on trying to end US support for a dictatorship in El Salvador. At that time, when I spoke to people about it, most said they had no idea what was going on. This was strange and confusing to me as there was much news coverage of the war. I had a strong sense that people had found a way to cultivate a not knowing, and that our political work was not so much about giving information as it was about working through those mechanisms of denial.

At the end of the Second World War, Karl Jaspers challenged the German people to come to a healthy relationship to the responsibilities they bore for the holocaust and the war. Many Germans had themselves been through harrowing experiences as their government began to lose the war, some had actively opposed the Nazi regime, and even more had not been actively engaged in supporting it. And yet after the war, the rest of the world held the Germans collectively responsible for the horrors of Nazism. This led many Germans to feel resentful as they saw themselves as victims of circumstances beyond their control.

Before the war, Jaspers was a prominent German philosophy professor, a gentile with a Jewish wife. Because of his wife's heritage, during the war Jaspers lost his ability to teach, and both were in constant fear for their lives. They carried cyanide pills at all times, to be prepared for the necessity of suicide. And yet both survived the Nazi period living in Germany.

In a series of lectures, delivered right after the war, and published under the title *The Question of German Guilt*, he distinguished four types of guilt: criminal, political, moral, and metaphysical. Working with this typology he then went on to help Germans who survived the war come to terms with their positions, and find a way forward as a people.

He argued that people carry criminal guilt when they themselves were involved with actions that were capable of objective proof and in violation of laws. The people in positions of relative power within the Nazi regime were clearly criminal. Their guilt and liability for punishment were not hard to understand. And their punishment was to be expected.

Below the level of criminal liability, was the realm of moral guilt, a sense of responsibility for acting as good people should act. Each person would have to search their own conscience to decide if they carried moral guilt. Each of us is morally responsible for the actions we take and the ones we avoid. No one but ourselves can judge us here.

For moral guilt, the court is our own conscience. During the war many people acted in cowardly ways and did not protect others, or resist when it was possible to resist. No one should be punished for that cowardice, but each person should look into themselves and ask if they did what they could to live ethically in that challenging time, and come to terms as an individual with that knowledge.[21]

In exploring moral guilt, Jaspers asked that each person reflect for themselves on what they did and did not do to protect the victims of Nazism and to challenge the regime.

> Passivity knows itself morally guilty of every failure, every neglect to act whenever possible, to shield the imperiled, to relieve the wrong, to countervail. Impotent submission always left a margin of activity which, though not without risk, could still be cautiously effective. Its anxious omission weighs upon the individual as moral guilt. Blindness for the misfortune of others, lack of imagination of the heart, inner indifference toward the witnessed evil—that is moral guilt.[22]

Political guilt, on the other hand, was a concept he created to make sense of the collective responsibility that the German people bore as a whole, no matter what their relationship to the Nazi regime. Here he argues that modern politics requires that we must each bear the consequences of the deeds of the state whose power governs us. Everybody is co-responsible for the way he is governed.

People cannot be held criminally liable for this sort of guilt, but they can be held responsible for the actions of the community in which they find themselves.

> Political liberty begins with the majority of individuals in a people feeling jointly liable for the politics of their community.... Politics looks in the concrete world for the negotiable path of each day, guided by the idea of human existence as liberty.[23]

He argued that political and moral guilt are enmeshed in the question of how we are morally obligated to work for more just political systems.

> Every human being is fated to be enmeshed in the power relations he [sic] lives by. This is the inevitable guilt of all, the guilt of human existence.... Failure to collaborate in organizing power relations, in the struggle for power for the sake of serving the right, creates basic political guilt and moral guilt at the same time.... For wherever power does not limit itself, there exists violence and terror, and in the end the destruction of life and soul.[24]

Because the Germans as a people bore political guilt, it made sense for the world to expect the new German state to make amends for what happened and for the German people as a whole to pay for those amends. Political guilt is a practical reality of living in nation-states. By distinguishing the political reality from criminal and moral guilt, Jaspers is able to ask the German people to step up to some level of responsibility, without that responsibility implying anything about their own personal goodness or liability to punishment.

The final category he lays out is metaphysical guilt. Here, he argues that

> there exists a solidarity among men [sic] as human beings that makes each co-responsible for every wrong and every injustice

in the world, especially for crimes committed in his presence or with his knowledge. If I fail to do whatever I can to prevent them, I too am guilty. If I was present at the murder of others without risking my life to prevent it, I feel guilty in a way not adequately conceivable either legally, politically, or morally.[25]

Jasper's concept of metaphysical guilt says that none of us can have a totally happy consciousness when we live in a world where others suffer unnecessarily. It isn't possible to have a complete sense of moral well-being in a world where we are all connected and where terribly unjust things are happening to people. Jaspers is not asking us to have feelings of shame and self-loathing. Jaspers argues that metaphysical guilt should throw us into a state of humility. Humility—the opposite of arrogance—is a state of being deeply open to rethinking one's basic ways of being and sense of identity. That humility requires openness to the horrors of the world, and a commitment to live well and ethically in the face of those horrors.[26]

Jaspers's categories can be helpful for understanding the moral predicament that we all face as people living in a deeply unjust and deeply connected modern world. Perpetrators of criminal acts need to be held criminally liable. Citizens should feel a sense of responsibility for the actions of their governments, and see it as their responsibility to act in ways that make the governments under which they live act justly, and not be surprised when others hold them responsible for the actions of those governments.

That leaves us with a fundamentally ambiguous approach to ethics. There are no certain rules or clearly defined paths for action. And there is no way to live with a clear sense of moral purity. In *The Ethics of Ambiguity* Simone de Beauvoir argues that in the absence of some absolute and clear given set of rules for behavior, we are all responsible for our actions,

> because man [sic] is abandoned on the earth, because his acts are definitive, absolute engagements. He bears the responsibility for a world which is not the work of a strange power, but of himself, where his defeats are inscribed, & his victories as well.[27]

The existentialist philosophers Jaspers and de Beauvoir argue that each of us should reflect on our actions and refusals to act and find ways to build a good life that involves consistency with our own beliefs about how the world should be. We need to adopt an attitude of humility that is open to the tragedy of living together in a world filled with injustices to which we are all connected and which we have some ability to impact, but where none of us has any certainty about which actions are the right ones.

Responsibility

> responsible: 2 Answerable, accountable, (to); liable to be called to account, having authority or control, being the cause. . . 3 Capable of fulfilling an obligation or trust, reliable trustworthy, of good credit, social position or reputation.

Iris Marion Young encourages us to not allow our ethical thinking to get stuck in issues of legal liability or guilt. Instead, she argues for a focus on the concept of responsibility.

> The point is not to blame, punish, or seek redress from those who did it, but rather to enjoin those who participate by their actions in the process of collective action to change it.[28]

We have an ethical obligation to understand the ways we are connected and to think of how we can be part of the process of building a better world. When we take responsibility and hold others responsible, we should be mindful of what we are trying to accomplish with the idea of responsibility.

According to Anthony Lang, in an article on preventing genocide, there are four reasons to hold an agent responsible for something that is seen as violating a social norm: (1) the communication of a statement to set the record straight and clarify society's morals, (2) to stop the violation from happening by setting up a system of deterrence, (3) to establish "some level of justice by ensuring that the agent held responsible suffers in some way for the violation of the norm," and (4) to reform the agent so it doesn't happen again.[29]

Punishment is one of a number of ways to hold an agent accountable. Sometimes giving voice is enough to change the system for the better and to make an injustice not happen again, it can set up moral values that dissuade. When evaluating the ways we need to hold others responsible, it is always important to keep within our view what we are trying to accomplish, and how that imposition of responsibility will have a real impact on the systems of power we are trying to hold to account.

When we are open to our responsibilities, we see our connections to the complex and fraught social fabric we inhabit. We can see the many actions we can take to transform that world. It can be emotionally overwhelming to live in awareness of the thousands of things that cause pain in our deeply connected world. It can be exhausting to see all of the things that one could do but chooses not to. But it can also be deeply satisfying to feel the ways that one's actions are part of the healing of the social fabric we inhabit. And it is possible to build a life that is aware, engaged, and also full of enough joy, pleasure, and rest, to make that engagement sustainable.

The way for individuals to act ethically in a connected and fragmented world is to go beyond individualism, and to see themselves as co-responsible for a fabric of connections. The way to a just political system is to work to foster equal power relations that will lead to a healthy social fabric.

3
Democracy in Crisis

The Greeks got themselves into that whole mess, with their corrupt government and overspending. Why should everyone else have to pay for their laziness and bad choices? They need to take responsibility and pay back the money they borrowed. Since the Greek people voted for the governments that took out those loans, they are responsible for paying them back. [1]

The Greek people work more hours than the Germans. This whole thing about the Greeks lying around on the beaches and drinking is a total fabrication. It's people from the rich countries who lie on Greek beaches and in the evenings get served their liquor by those Greeks. The Greek people elected Tsipras, and Tsipras was supposed to represent them. The banks made bad investments and should have paid the consequences. Alexis Tsipras was a sellout. If he had held tight, and done what the voters voted him in for, we would have seen the beginning of the unravelling of the whole corrupt system. Why bother even electing someone like that?

Easy for you to say that. You wouldn't be the one under the thumb of the masters of the world. The people of Greece would have been punished with no mercy. The leaders elected by your people are the ones who define boundaries of the stage on

which our leaders play their very small, somewhat pathetic, and almost always tragic parts.

Isn't that the way it goes? You elect some people, and they promise you the moon, and you think they are going to do right by you. But really, they'll always just play the tune for the one who pays the piper.

...

In many countries, support for democracy, understood as a government based on elections, is waning.[2] In some cases, this is because of the ways that government officials are bought by monied interests. In other cases, even well-meaning elected officials aren't able to deliver what their constituents ask for, because the resources that those constituents need are anchored in processes over which national governments don't have much control.

The growing crisis in democracy can be seen as a result of the more general crisis in accountability. As destructive powers run rampant across the globe, faith that we can live well, if we elect government officials who will manage society in our interests, is waning. Many of the authors writing about the crisis of democracy have powerful insights about some aspect of the problems we face, but this literature is generally flawed by underestimating the seriousness of the crisis of accountability in which this crisis of democracy is embedded.

In *The People vs. Democracy: Why Our Freedom Is in Danger and How to Save It*, Yascha Mounk argues that there are three major social changes that are undermining the stability of the current system in many nominally liberal democratic countries: the rise of social media; people's lowered optimism about their, and their children's, economic futures; and a decline in ethnic unity in many nation-states.

Mounk argues that we are entering a period where transformed means of communication are destabilizing settled social patterns. As social media replaces the book's "one to many" form of communication with a network of "many to many" modes of communication, the gatekeepers who had ensured stability in the systems of meaning, through control of publishing, have given way to a system of almost unrestrained communication. He argues that, for all of its faults, "the dominance of mass media limited the distribution of extreme ideas, created a set of shared facts and values, and slowed the spread of fake news."[3] Social media is changing all of that, leading to deep instability, with both good and bad outcomes.

Through the stable period experienced in the United States and Western Europe since the Second World War, many countries saw rising living standards, and a sense that the future would be better than the past. This kept people in those countries happy enough with their political systems to not rock the boat. As economic growth has slowed and economic inequality has risen, many people have a sense that their futures and their children's futures are likely to be worse than the past. And many blame their governments and politicians for not delivering.

Finally, most of the world's stable liberal democracies have been relatively mono-ethnic. The European nation-states were mostly built on the basis of one dominant ethnic group. The United States was built upon a dominant white identity, even if that white group was drawn from a variety of "nations." As people of color in the United States are moving toward a majority status, many white Americans are vulnerable to the rhetoric of nativist politicians.

A lot of the anger at immigration is driven by fear of an imagined future rather than displeasure with a lived reality. When immigration levels rise, it is not so much the experience of day to day life that changes; more important is a change in the social imaginary of what the country's future might hold. As a result, the belief that people from the majority group will eventually be in the minority plays a dominant role in the political imagination of the far right both in Western Europe and in North America. And generally, it is people with less actual contact with those "others," who have the most negative fears.[4]

The nativist fears incited by politicians in democratic countries can lead liberal democracies to turn into what Fareed Zakaria calls "illiberal democracy." For him, an illiberal democracy is a country that has regular elections, but few constitutional protections for opposition parties. In these countries, the media is controlled by the party in power; opposition party members are threatened, jailed, or killed; and protest movements are suppressed, such that the people in power are able to maintain their power, unchecked by the formal processes of elections. This sort of system is presently operating in Turkey, Hungary, Poland, Zimbabwe, and Russia, to name just a few.

These countries are democratic in the very narrow sense that they have elections, but are illiberal in the sense that they don't have strong constitutional protections for individuals or opposition political parties, media, and movements.[5] Robert Kuttner says this term gives them too much credit, and really there is nothing democratic about the electoral systems of these countries. He prefers to call them "neofascist."[6]

Part of what leads to the undermining of support for liberal democracy, which can lead to illiberal democracy, or neofascism, is that many liberal democracies are so controlled by money in their electoral systems, that the will of the people is not expressed through elections. Collin Crouch writes,

> Under this model, while elections certainly exist and can change governments, public electoral debate is a tightly controlled

spectacle, managed by rival teams of professionals, expert in the techniques of persuasion, and considering a small range of issues selected by those teams. The mass of citizens plays a passive, quiescent, even apathetic part, responding only to the signals given them. Behind this spectacle of the electoral game, politics is really shaped in private by interaction between elected governments and elites that overwhelmingly represent business interests.[7]

In some European countries, such as Greece, France, Spain, and Italy, old political parties which had ruled since the end of the Second World War have suddenly lost so much support that very new parties, or extreme right-wing nationalist parties, which until recently, had been very marginal, suddenly are taking large numbers of votes and shaking up what had been very stable systems. In Europe, national sovereignty has been limited by the large aspects of political life that are controlled by the European Union, which is increasingly run according to technocratic rather than democratic principles.[8]

Mounk calls this technocratic approach to governance "undemocratic liberalism," where institutions function without input or response to the concerns of the governed, and yet the basic constitutional protections, which define "liberalism," remain in place. Monk focuses his description of undemocratic liberalism on the European Union, where a set of institutions controlled by an elite group is able to make powerful decisions, such as imposing austerity on the people of Greece, without being accountable to a functioning democratic process. Frustrations with undemocratic liberalism can often throw a population into the arms of the nativist politicians who push for illiberal democracy. This is much of the story behind the Brexit vote in the United Kingdom, and the 2016 election in the United States.

Critics on the left, from at least the time of Marx, have argued that formal democratic processes embedded in a capitalist economic structures, leave us with a political system prone to be run by and for elites. If there is no democracy in the economic sphere, then political systems are prone to being corrupted or insignificant.

In *Can Democracy Survive Global Capitalism?*, Robert Kuttner argues that an electoral system in a capitalist context needs intense protections to keep the wealthy from dominating politics through control over media, and spending in elections.

> In some idealized world, capitalism may enhance democracy, but in the history of the West, democracy has expanded by *limiting* the power of capitalists. When that project fails, dark forces are often unleashed. In the twentieth century, capitalism coexisted with dictatorships, which conveniently create friendly business climates and repress independent worker organizations.[9]

As globalization has intensified, this problem of maintaining democracy in the face of capitalism has become more difficult. According to Kuttner,

> The fact that the far-right backlash is occurring in nearly all Western nations at the same time is no coincidence, nor is it accidental contagion. It is a common reaction against the impact of globalization on the livelihoods of ordinary people.[10]

If we want to protect society from the rise of illiberal democracy, or neofascism, we need to take very seriously what it would mean to make society democratic in ways that give people control over their lives. We need to do more than allow them to vote for the technocrats who would extract wealth from them. Undemocratic liberalism is not just an unfortunate state of affairs. It is precisely the problem that leads voters in Western "democracies" to choose illiberal democracy. And the way to fight it is not just to wring our hands, and suggest that those with power act more responsibly. The fight for democracy is not just a fight for formal politics. It is also a fight for control over all of the forms of unaccountable power that dominate our lives. We address the crisis in democracy best by addressing the crisis in accountability.

Freedom from Domination by Destructive Powers

We are entering a period where the social structures and mechanisms that have channeled and controlled power for the past few hundred years are shifting radically. The need to develop systems of accountability to tame those operations of power is urgent.

In *The End of Power: From Boardrooms to Battlefields and Churches to States: Why Being in Charge Isn't What It Used to Be*, former Venezuelan politician and former director of the World Bank, Moisés Naím, describes some serious ways that the systems we have lived under since the Second World War are becoming deeply unstable. He argues that there are three deep social transformations which have undermined old barriers to new forces gaining power—he calls these transformations *more*, *mobility*, and *mentality*. The fact that there are many more of us than there used to be has led to systems of control being overwhelmed. There are more people in the world, who are generally living longer and doing better than in past times. This is leading people all around the world to have rising expectations. "When people are more numerous and living fuller lives, they become more difficult to regimen and control."[11]

With mobility, cultures are being disrupted by mass migration. Where in prior years, there was pervasive problem of a brain drain, as educated people left countries of the Global South and took their expensive educations with them, increasingly there is a "brain circulation," where those people are returning to their countries of origin and bringing with them new ideas, and access to capital.

Ideals of how it is possible to live, circulate freely, and information about possible solutions to problems also circulate with increasing freedom and speed. With the mentality revolution, people all around the world, and especially young people, are thinking for themselves and questioning the traditional expectations of their societies.

While Naím argues that what is happening is an end to power, what he very aptly describes is more like a destabilization of old structures and a shifting of power. In terms of culture, Naím sees the undermining of traditional cultures in almost entirely positive terms, as an unleashing of people's senses of possibility. But, of course, along with the undermining of traditional cultures comes the spreading of capitalist forms of culture and that can be seen as the spread of newer forms of power as much as it can be seen as the undermining of old ones.

Naím's book can be seen as an elegy for what William Robinson calls the transnational ruling class. From the end of the Second World War, until very recently, transnational institutions such as the World Trade Organization, the International Monetary Fund, and the World Bank were able to control the rules under which the economies of the world functioned. And their power was so great that any national government that wanted to do things according to a different set of rules would be denied access to the capital needed to keep its economy functioning. Any country that tried something different would be pressured until it played by the political and economic rules determined by those institutions. The transnational ruling class had enormous power over both economic and political systems. That system extracted wealth from the Global South, and kept many countries from moving their populations out of poverty. But they also kept the global system quite stable.

Robinson argues that the last part of the twentieth century was characterized by a system of polyarchy where power came to transcend national governments and instead rested in the hands of a transnational ruling class and its governing institutions. He argues that national elections became not as significant as they once had been as mechanisms for deciding how people live.

We can see this problem in action in the dramatic situation faced by the government of Greece in the summer of 2015. Prior to the financial bubble bursting in 2008, Goldman Sachs and others had pressured a corrupt Greek government into taking out a set of very unsustainable loans. When the global economy crashed, those who had made risky loans could have borne the results of those risks, and lost their money. Instead, transnational institutions pressured the Greek people to make good on the loans.

The Greek government fell, and was replaced by a left-wing government led by what had been until that time a tiny and obscure party, Syriza. Syriza's Alexis Tsipras came to power on a platform of rejecting the loans as illegitimate. The European Central Bank insisted that Greece not default. What followed was a very dramatic set of moves that showed how little power the people of Greece had over their political and economic reality.

Tsipras considered the loans to be illegitimate and unpayable. German finance minister Wolfgang Schäuble insisted on Greece's repayment, and threatened to cut off all capital to Greece if they didn't pay. Schäuble famously said that "elections change nothing." He led the charge of the European Central Bank in insisting that Greece squeeze more capital out of its economy by cutting pensions, raising taxes, and selling off national assets.

Looking for more power at the negotiating table, Tsipras held a referendum on whether or not the Greeks wanted to accept the deal. The Greek people voted with a resounding "Oxi" or no, and Tsipras went back to the negotiating table with more power. The institutions backed off somewhat and countered with a deal that still forced austerity on the Greek people, but which was slightly less bad.

Tsipras was faced with an impossible choice: accept a deal that would be devastating to the people of Greece, and for which they had just indicated opposition through the election, or leave the Eurozone. Polls had shown that the people of Greece were actually not in favor of leaving the Eurozone. Tsipras "chose" to accept the deal.[12]

As the head of a national government, Greece's Alexis Tsipras looks like an agent when he chooses to call for a referendum and when he decides to cut a deal with the European banks. But like the protagonist of a Greek tragedy, Tsipras was up against an impossible fate. Contemporary Western narratives tend to favor the trope of the heroic individual who comes in to save the day. The way Western thinkers tend to look at the world, in our narrative systems, as well as in our political and moral philosophies, tends to focus on the foreground of individual actors, and tend to not see the background of the context in which choices are made.

Tsipras's choices were emergent properties of a set of relations much bigger than himself. If we see how embedded we are all are in a social fabric, then it becomes clearer that we need to be held responsible not just for those actions that appear as free decisions but also for all of the ways we weave the social fabric and reproduce social realities.

This makes all of us, from Tsipras to German finance minister Schäuble, to you and I, at the same time more responsible and also less responsible than we are accustomed to thinking. More, because as Iris Marion Young says, we bear some responsibility for the social processes we enact and for the results of those social processes. And less, because our actions are not as free and unconstrained as they sometimes appear to be. Our actions are all emergent properties of complex and interrelated systems.

National governments are officially in charge of what happens in their territory, but increasingly, since the second half of the twentieth century, governments have been under tremendous pressure to follow the rules set by transnational institutions. Those institutions largely see their job as making the world safe for routine profitmaking and protecting the liberty of the world's major multinational corporations.

And yet, Naím is partially right, we do seem to be entering a period in which the ability of the transnational ruling class to provide an orderly atmosphere in which entrenched interests operate is crumbling. But the capitalist processes, which destroy people's lives, are as powerful as ever.[13]

What has changed is that those capitalist processes are less able to be managed by a cohesive transnational ruling class, and they are less accountable to any particular regime of control. The World Bank and International Monetary Fund, and other transnational institutions are less able to manage global capital, as finance capital becomes increasingly dominant, and as there is less consensus among elites about how it should function.[14]

Naím seems right that the power of individuals at the heads of major corporations, or as the heads of transnational institutions does seem to be destabilizing. The forms of power that he and people like him have held in the past century, the power of heads of corporations, the powers of people in government, and the powers of people at the head of transnational organizations, is shifting, and those people can no longer feel secure in their ability make things happen.

And yet the configuration of power concentrated in transnational capitalist processes is an increasingly important part of what rules the world. It is just ruling in a less orderly fashion. Part of this shift has to do with a change in the relationships between nations, as countries of the Global South become more prominent economic players, and as Asia is increasingly displacing Europe and the United States as the dominant force in global economic processes.

In *Multipolar Globalization Emerging Economies and Development,* Jan Nederveen Pieterse argues that

> the old core-periphery relations no longer hold. The global South no longer looks just north, but also sideways. East Asian development models have long overtaken Western prescription. South-South cooperation, heralded as an alternative to dependence on the West ever since the Bandung Movement of Non-aligned countries (1955), is now taking shape.[15]

He claims that in 2013, 58 percent of global trade took place between countries of the Global South.[16] New South-South trading partnerships, as well as alternative institutions for offering finance capital, are emerging outside the old network of the Western based institutions such as the World Bank and International Monetary Fund.

In their 1848 *Communist Manifesto,* Marx and Engels highlight the ways that, as economic processes spread that allow for the free flow of capital to wherever it is likely to get the greatest return, there goes with that a tremendous destabilization of society, along with intermittent attempts to manage the ensuing chaos. In one of the most oft quoted passages in the *Manifesto*, they write,

> Constant revolutionizing of production, uninterrupted disturbance of all social conditions, everlasting uncertainty and agitation distinguish the bourgeois epoch from all earlier ones. All fixed, fast-frozen relations, with their train of ancient and venerable prejudices and opinions are swept away, all new-formed ones become antiquated before they can ossify. All that is solid melts into air, all that is holy is profaned.[17]

Rather than being in a period of an end to power, we are in yet another period of an unmooring of power and therefore another period of a rising crisis of accountability. The old systems that have managed collective decision-making in the near past have been undermined. Support for democracy is likely to continue to wane if nominally democratic governments are not able to deliver for people a sense of well-being. And increasingly that well-being is being undermined by a variety of configurations of power which are not being held to account. We need robust forces challenging and holding to account the dangerous powers that dominate our lives. One way out of the crisis of democracy is to broaden what we mean by that concept. Democracy needs to be unleashed from its limitation to the election of people to run governments. The *demos*, or the people, need to find ways to make it such that they are running society in meaningful ways, and holding to account the powers that wreaking havoc on our lives.

4

Politics beyond the Polis, Democracy beyond Elections

I love the ideal of democracy. If people could get together and talk and argue in civil and respectful ways, we would be able to solve these problems. I imagine the best of Athenian democracy as what we should be trying for. [1]

The last thing I want is to sit around and talk with people like you all day. I believe in freedom. I don't want the government to take what I have. What I mostly want is to be left alone. It's up to you to make something of your life. I hate when people whine and ask the government to solve their problems.

You are not free when the government leaves you alone and corporations destroy our communities. You don't know a thing about the nature of freedom. You're afraid of big government, well I'm afraid of big corporations. And I am not free when they are able to destroy the atmosphere. I am not even bothering with elections. I put my energy into taking down the system that gives corporations the power to destroy our lives.

The elections that happen in your countries have so much more impact on my life than the ones in which I'm able to vote. You elect the rulers who determine whether or not people in my country have access to credit and what the temperature will be in the future. We all live with the consequences of your elections. I remain committed to voting whenever I get the chance. It is one small piece of power I have, and I exercise it to the best of my ability.

Politics is such an ugly game. I want nothing to do with it. It's just a bunch of people looking for power. I always vote, because my people died fighting for that right. But I never seem to be offered a politician who will actually make a difference in the things that matter to me. Beyond doing that duty, I'd rather stay as far from politics as I possibly can.

Politics

> political: 1 Of belonging to, or concerned with, the form, organization, and administration of a State, or part of a State, and with the regulations of its relations with other States; of or pertaining to public life and affairs as involving authority and governments
>
> *polis*: Gk= city
>
> state: Commonwealth, polity; commonweal.

In the West, there are two dominant views of politics that live, often jumbled together, in our imaginations. According to one, grounded in ancient Greek ideals, politics is rooted in the imagery of the small cohesive community. In his book *Politics*, Aristotle outlined the principles for how people should live together well in an independent society, community, or a polis. Much of how we think about democracy is rooted in the idea of that cohesive community being self-governing by the people as a whole.

The other view grew out of the Enlightenment, and owes much to John Locke. On that view, the job of politics is to create a framework for individuals to keep out of each other's ways. It sets up national governments which protect private property and individual rights, in order to allow for a maximum of autonomy for the sovereign individual.

In the present period, where the powers that impact our lives are spread across the whole planet, embedded in our systems of meaning, and in our senses of self, we need to shift how we think about the nature of politics, and about the nature of democracy. Some of that shift will require ridding our thinking of the destructive forms of individualism and pro-market thinking that underlie the Enlightenment view. The other challenge will be to adapt the Aristotelian view to a global scale.

In *Undoing the Demos: Neoliberalism's Stealth Revolution*, Wendy Brown argues that the ancient Greek ideal and Enlightenment modernity are each based on a different way of understanding what it means to be human. *Homo oeconomicus* is the human being understood as a self-interested agent, maximizing her own gain and living in a world dominated by market logics. She contrasts this character with *homo politicus*, or the human being understood as "a language-using, moral, and associational creature who utilizes these capacities to govern himself [or her or themselves] with others."[2] Brown argues that we need to bring *homo politicus* back into how we understand politics. She harkens back to the political ideals of Aristotle, who saw human beings as *homo politicus*.

This view of government was common in Western political theory before it was eclipsed by thinkers such as Locke. This older tradition saw people as fundamentally social animals, and understood the project of politics to be how we figure out how to live well together. That older tradition is sometimes referred to as republicanism. The terms *republican*, *democratic*, and *liberal* all have meanings in political theory that stretch and shift in ways very different from how they are used in contemporary politics. In the context of political theory, a democrat is one who is especially interested in the rule of the people, whereas a republican is more interested in the rule of law and a constitution. Liberalism is the political philosophy that is focused on individual liberty.

> republican: 2A Of, belonging to or characteristic of a republic; having the form or constitution of a republic.
>
> republic: 2 Any state in which supreme power is held by the people or their elected representatives as opp. to by a monarch etc.; a constitution.
>
> democratic: 1. Government by the people; a form of government in which the power resides in the people and is exercised by them either directly or by means of elected representatives.
>
> liberalism: 5. Favorable to or respectful of individual rights and freedoms.

In his book *Republicanism: A Theory of Freedom in Government*, political theorist Philip Pettit calls for a revival of the republican tradition which draws on the thinking of Aristotle, Cicero, Machiavelli, and Hamilton. That tradition, he claims, puts an

> emphasis on having certain institutions in place: for example, an empire of law and not, as it was often put, not an empire

of men; a mixed constitution, in which different powers serve to check and balance each other; and a regime of civic virtue, under which people are disposed to serve, and serve honestly, in public office.[3]

And, he argues, the most important thread in this tradition is the way it conceives of liberty. The liberal tradition of Locke and Jefferson sees liberty as freedom from interference, so that one is free when one is left alone by government to do pretty much as one pleases in the worlds of business and home. The person who deserves liberty is usually imagined as a property-owning free male and never as an enslaved person or a woman. One of the most important liberties Jefferson wanted was the freedom to own slaves without being infringed upon by a meddling government.

In his book *Hamilton* (which inspired the Broadway play of the same name), historian Ron Chernow asks us to rethink how we evaluate the US founding fathers Alexander Hamilton and Thomas Jefferson. This leads to a rethinking of how we evaluate the republican versus the democratic traditions within US history, how we think about the nature of liberty, and how we understand the role of government in limiting power.[4] Chernow goes too far in his positive evaluation of Hamilton, who was responsible for some of the more elitist aspects of the US constitution. And yet his view is an important corrective to the standard evaluations of these traditions within the US system.[5]

Speaking of Jefferson and his allies, Chernow writes,

> Many of these slaveholding populists were celebrated by posterity as tribunes of the common people. Meanwhile, the self-made Hamilton, a fervent abolitionist and a staunch believer in meritocracy, was villainized in American history as an apologist of privilege and wealth.[6]

In the dominant narrative, Jefferson's slaveholding is often seen (as is John Locke's engagement with slavery) as no more than an embarrassing personal inconsistency. Chernow makes a powerful case that Jefferson's populism was often demagoguery used to protect his privileges as a slave-owner.

In the republican tradition, freedom is defined as being free from domination, rather than as being free from interference. Thus, the goal of politics is to develop a good society which works for the needs of all, and which provides mechanisms for protection from domination, at home, in business, and in relation to government.

Pettit argues that this republican tradition was strong among Western political theorists until around the time of the US and French Revolutions, when larger groups of people were asking to be part of the political realm. The republican notion of liberty as freedom from domination

> went out of fashion only as it became clear, towards the end of the eighteenth century, that with citizenship extended beyond the realm of propertied males, it was no longer possible to think of making all citizens free in the old sense; in particular it was not feasible, under received ideas, to think of conferring freedom as non-domination on women and servants. If freedom was to be cast as an ideal for all citizens, then freedom would have to be reconceived in less demanding terms.[7]

For Pettit, Machiavelli is one of the most important theorists of republicanism. Paraphrasing Machiavelli, Pettit writes, "The law-giver has to make pessimistic assumptions about people in positons of power; vis. 'that they are always going to act according to the wickedness of their spirits whenever they have free scope.' "[8] The goal of a just political system is to find mechanisms that limit the accumulation of power. Machiavelli was especially concerned with the ways that wealth leads to political power and thus, unless checked, will destroy a republic.

Pettit finds concepts in republicanism that are helpful for understanding how a political system can challenge domination.

> Liberalism has been associated for over the two hundred years of its development, and in most of its influential varieties, with the negative conception of freedom as the absence of interference, and with the assumption that there is nothing inherently oppressive about some people having dominating power over others, provided they do not exercise that power and are not likely to exercise it. This relative indifference to power or domination has made liberalism tolerant of relationships in the home, in the workplace, in the electorate, and elsewhere, that the republican must denounce as paradigms of domination and unfreedom.[9]

Liberal political theory says that everyone must have a vote in the political system and that everyone should be left alone as much as possible. Outside the scope of vision of liberal political theory are the webs of relations that connect us. The liberal tradition has trouble arguing for the state to do anything to check the unjust actions of men over their wives or employers over employees.

In both of those cases, government intervention is seen as problematic, overstepping of limited the role the state is supposed to have in just protecting people from interference in the public sphere. Pettit argues that most contemporary liberals believe in protection against domestic abuse as well as protection against workplace abuse. But, he argues, they need to go somewhere other than the liberal political tradition to find arguments for the rightness of challenges to those behaviors.

Pettit is arguing for a way of seeing politics as a set of practices that increase our freedom, by asking that our political institutions help to undermine domination. By focusing on ways to limit the accumulation of power, the republican tradition focuses on creating systems of accountability in government.

Two basic assumptions underlying the republican tradition are that in human social systems, there is always the possibility of power accumulating, and in any system of government, because governments are sites where power is concentrated, the power within government needs to be checked. Classical republicans argue for the rule of law to check arbitrary uses of power. They argue for systems of checks and balances, so that government will not become an unjust source of power itself, and they argue for the importance of an engaged citizenry so that people will feel enough a part of the political process that they will work to keep the system accountable and will use that power to challenge forms of domination.

The republican tradition offers the idea of freedom as freedom from domination, and a return to *homo politicus* as the agent of politics. Brown argues that with the move toward a more technocratic society where *homo oeconomicus* is replacing *homo politicus*, there are fewer places where political decisions of the people are significant for determining how we live.

In a world where we are all connected on a global scale, our view of the political needs to take into consideration all the configurations of power that impact our lives as well as the mechanisms of governance, or administration, that regulate those systems. Democracy needs to be about both how people come to decide and how those systems should operate. The republican tradition was developed to understand the nature of power in discrete localities, and these ideas need to be broadened in some significant ways if they are to help us understand how to hold de-territorialized forms of power to account.

Accountability Democracy

In *The Good Citizen*, Michael Schudson argues that beginning in the mid-twentieth century, there has been a shift in how democracy functions. Speaking of the electoral system in the United States, Schudson argues that

> we can say that the "ownership" of the political sphere has shifted. In the eighteenth century, political activity was set in motion and controlled by gentlemen; in the nineteenth century, it was organized by parties; in the twentieth century, after democratization had reduced the authority of social class and reform had seriously weakened the parties, multiple claimants compete to set the standards of political life. The media, political candidates set adrift from party, the increasingly important, well-funded and professionally staffed interest groups, the government bureaucracies shielded in many respects from close public scrutiny, and individual citizens empowered by the expansion of "rights" all bid to define what counts as politics and what the experience of politics might mean.[10]

He argues that "the ideal of the 'informed citizen,' arose in the Progressive Era as part of a broad-gauge attack on the power of political parties." But, he says, this ideal is being displaced by a new ideal of the rights-bearing citizen.[11] As people increasingly advocate for things like safe products and an end to domestic violence, the wall between the personal and the political becomes less clear. Increasingly people are working to advocate for their rights in areas that in the recent past were not considered to be political issues.[12]

And, whereas in the era of the informed citizen, the ideal citizen was one who paid a lot of attention to what elected officials were doing, and found elections to be the most important aspect of civic life about which to be informed, our era requires something different of a good citizen.

The good citizen of the current period is characterized as a "rights-bearing" or "monitorial" citizen. These citizens scan (rather than read) the informational environment in a way so that they may be alerted on a very wide variety of issues for a very wide variety of ends and may be mobilized around these issues in a large variety of ways.... Picture parents watching small children at the community pool. They are not gathering information; they are keeping an eye on the scene. They look inactive, but they are poised for action if action is required. The monitorial citizen is not an absentee citizen but watchful, even while he or she is doing something else. Citizenship during a particular political season may be for many people much less intense than in the era of parties, but citizenship is now a year-round and day-long activity, as it was only rarely in the past.[13]

Drawing heavily on Schudson's work, in his book the *Life and Death of Democracy*, John Keane argues that beginning around the middle of the twentieth century there was a proliferation of challenges to power, which existed outside the structures of formal representative democracy, working to contest domination through an increasingly wide array of mechanisms.

He argues that as social systems become more complex, the way to keep society democratic was transformed to being anchored in checking unjust accumulations of power. Democracy in this period needs to be more about limiting the power of others than it is about giving us each a voice as an individual within a national government.

The years since 1945 have seen the invention of about a hundred different types of power-monitoring devices that never before existed within the world of democracy. These watchdog and guide-dog and barking-dog inventions are changing both the political geography and the political dynamics of many democracies, which no longer bear much resemblance to textbook models of representative democracy, which supposed that citizens' needs are

> best championed through elected parliamentary representatives chosen by political parties. . . . These extra-parliamentary power-monitoring institutions include—to mention at random just a few—public integrity commissions, judicial activism, local courts, workplace tribunals, consensus conferences, parliaments for minorities, public interest litigation, citizens' juries, citizens' assemblies, independent public inquiries, think-tanks, experts' reports, participatory budgeting, vigils, "blogging" and other novel forms of media scrutiny.[14]

Keane argues that direct democracy makes sense in a society that communicates face to face. Representative democracy is associated with the printed word. Our increasingly networked society, with forms of communication branching in all directions, and connecting people in a variety of increasingly fast and efficient ways, needs another form of democracy. He calls this new emerging form *monitory democracy*.

> Monitory democracy is tied closely to the growth of multi-media-saturated societies—societies whose structures of power are continuously "bitten" by monitory institutions operating within a new galaxy of media defined by the ethos of communicative abundance.[15]

Keane quotes the director of Mazlumder, a Turkish human rights organization, as arguing that monitory mechanisms and principles are more fundamental than representative democracy.

> Among the paradoxes of democracy is that people in one country can vote in a government that then does things that destroy the rights of people in that same country, or of other countries. Free elections, multi-party systems and voting based on freedom of information are a good thing. But rights and the justice that flows from their protection are definitely prior to democracy in this sense.[16]

In *Counter-Democracy: Politics in an Age of Distrust*, Pierre Rosanvallon argues that even before there was formal democracy in Europe there were claims made by people for protection from the abuses of those with power. He calls this tradition of challenging power "counter-democracy," and he sees it as an important companion to the development of electoral systems of government.

> By "counter-democracy" I mean not the opposite of democracy but rather a form of democracy that reinforces the usual electoral democracy as a kind of buttress, a democracy of indirect powers disseminated throughout society—in other words, a durable democracy of distrust, which compliments the episodic democracy of the usual electoral representative system.[17]

Along with Schudson, he resists ideas that people in the present are less civically engaged than in some idealized past because they are less interested in elections.

> The number of people participating in strikes or demonstrations, signing petitions, and expressing collective solidarity in other ways suggests that the age is not one of political apathy and that the notion that people are increasingly withdrawing into the private sphere is not correct. It is better to say that citizenship has changed in nature rather than declined. There has been a simultaneous diversification of the *range, form*, and *targets* of political expression. As political parties eroded, various styles of advocacy groups and associations developed. Major institutions of representation and bargaining saw their roles diminish as ad hoc organizations proliferated. Citizens now have many ways of expressing their grievances and complaints other than voting.[18]

Schudson uses "rights based" and "monitorial" citizenship as names for the ideal way we relate to this shift in power and how we hold power to account. Keane follows Schudson's lead and refers to this as "monitory democracy." Rosanvallon argues that we need to look to "counter-democracy" as a supplement to electoral democracy.

Because the term "monitory" sounds too much like "monetary" and because "counter-democracy" sounds like we are giving up on "power of the people" which is what democracy means at its etymological roots, I prefer to use the term "accountability democracy" to talk about these emerging ways to challenge power.

We are in a period when these accountability seeking forms of democracy are becoming increasingly significant. Accountability democracy is the ability people have to check accumulations of power. It is the power of people to determine the circumstances under which they live. When we have accountability democracy, we have systems in place to keep power from accumulating in the hands of those people or processes that are destructive to the social fabric we all inhabit.

There are millions of projects in the world today that are working to challenge the large-scale, contested, slippery, and elusive configurations of power we face. We are all, in different ways, parts of the problems we are trying to solve, and can all in a variety of ways be parts of the solutions. In the present period, as our understanding of power is broadened, and as we also broaden our understanding of ways to challenge power, our ideas of how to keep a society working well for all also has to change. Politics becomes the study of these processes. Democracy becomes a question of how to build up and support the mechanisms that will challenge those configurations of power that are destructive of the social fabric. Citizenship comes to be about how each of us sees ourselves as a part of those processes, and takes action as responsible members of the connected, fragmented, and overlapping communities we inhabit.

Citizenship

> Citizen. 1. An inhabitant of a city or town; esp.one possessing civic rights, as a freeman, etc. 2. A member, native or naturalized, of a (usu. specified) State or Commonwealth.
>
> Civic. 2. Of or pertaining to a city; municipal; urban 3. Of or pertaining to citizenship.

Just as the idea of politics has its roots in the image of the polis, so the idea of citizenship has its roots in the image of a person who is a part of a city. Schudson, Rosanvallon, and Keane, all argue for understanding citizenship beyond the limits of liberal electoral democracy. And yet, what does it mean to be a "citizen" in a political reality that is not grounded in a place?

When we imagine the person who participates in a democracy, we often imagine someone living in the Athenian polis, arguing in public before a large crowd. It is common for advocates of democracy to value dialogue and deliberation and to claim that the *demos* do their job by acting together to decide how society should be. For Aristotle human beings realize their true potential as members of a polis, where they deliberate on their view of the good life.[19]

Following this tradition, Wendy Brown argued that a healthy political world is run by *homo politicus*, that is, a person understood as engaging with important questions about how we can best live together. She harkens back to Rousseau who argued that

> we are free, sovereign, and self-legislating only when we join with others to set the terms by which we live together. Those who remain slaves to instinct or to individual interest forsake both freedom and humanness as they surrender this sovereignty over themselves.[20]

Most people live under territorially based governments and so need as much as ever to learn to be responsible citizens of the states that govern us. But the things that need to be done to develop civic virtue in the broader sense, in which we are co-responsible to hold to account the range of configurations of power we face, require that we rethink the notion of citizenship. We need a shared sense of purpose about our roles in a wide variety of communities or networks; we need education about a broad range of issues, and the skills we need are skills at holding power to account, not just at deliberation in a public sphere or voting in elections.

In the republican ideal, members of a small community develop their shared sense of purpose by being in dialogue about their society and how they want it to be. People grow to have a sense of themselves within the culture of a place, and the place's culture shifts as people influence it. The process of developing a sense of belonging is more complicated and fraught for a territory the size of a nation-state than it is for a city state. And it is even more complicated for those who want to challenge de-territorialized operations of power.

In *Imagined Communities: Reflections on the Origin and Spread of Nationalism*, Benedict Anderson argued that people who live in state-level societies are often unified through an imagined community that develops through things like reading national newspapers and being educated in public schools.[21] That sense of belonging can be an incredibly powerful force in people's lives. Something similar is operating in the development of a common sense of purpose and concern for others at a global scale.

When Honduran environmental activist Berta Cáceres was murdered in 2016, as a result of her work protecting land from logging, people all around the world were outraged, and it led to many people being mobilized to fight against the forces that had her killed. That concern for Cáceres was cultivated through the fact that she had won the widely recognized Goldman Environmental Prize in 2015. The ideals embedded in the *Universal Declaration of Human Rights,* and work done by thousands of organizations to propagate its values, were also important for developing the values that underlay that outrage. Her murder was discussed in a wide range of news sources, all of which create an imagined community that links many of us in deep emotional ways to Berta Cáceres. The affective ties that create communities do not need to be anchored in a specific locality to be powerful and to motivate us to act with civic virtue.

Early in the twentieth century John Dewey argued, in *Democracy and Education,* that a strong system of public education was necessary to develop citizenship in members of a democratic society. He believed that in addition to helping develop a common sense of purpose, public education would develop the basic literacy in humanities and social sciences, needed to prepare people to be good citizens. His work was influential in developing civic education and the broadly humanistic aspect of the public-school system in the United States and other liberal states. That approach has been undermined in recent decades by the neoliberalization of education, which has seen students more as future workers than as future citizens. The struggle to keep those broader questions as part of public education continues to be a site of struggle in many liberal democracies.[22]

The education that is needed for accountability democracy to function is not something on a different order from what is required to develop citizens for a state, or for a city state. Rather, schools need to help students learn how global systems function, what people have done to challenge power, and what more can be done to hold power to account. Students need to learn to see themselves as sharing in the fate of others around the world.

In *Cultivating Humanity: A Classical Defense of Reform in Liberal Education*, Martha Nussbaum argued that we need to develop a sense of "world citizenship."

> Citizens who cultivate their humanity need . . . to see themselves as citizens of some local regional group—but also, and above all, as human beings bound to other human beings by ties of recognition and concern . . . . [Where] cultivating our humanity in a complex, interlocking world involves an understanding of the way common needs and aims are differently realized in different circumstances.[23]

This ideal has been criticized as being a bit too thin to mobilize the passions needed to get us to act with civic virtue.[24] There have been thin attempts at global citizenship which are vulnerable to this criticism. Immediately after the Second World War, many advocated renouncing nationality and developing one world government. Those same people advocated for a move to one global language, Esperanto. What seems misplaced in that attempt was the idea that a small group of people could decide on the meaning of our citizenship and create a language with no history, out of thin air. Also problematic was the idea that a world government could be held to account.

What Nussbaum is referring to, though, is something more grounded than that. She is arguing for education that builds on existing systems of meaning to develop in us a sense of a common humanity and shared fate. What pulls on people's passions about situations, such as the murder of Berta Cáceres, are less related to some abstract notion of global citizenship, than they are a set of overlapping concerns about human rights, about empathy for any human being, as well as a common sense of purpose in fighting for a better world. Those concerns have grown over a long period of time, in transnational social movements, in literature and other forms of art, and in transnational institutions, such as the United Nations. The systems of meaning that Nussbaum's world citizen inhabits have long and deep resonances. At this point in history, the systems of meaning that led to an outpouring of concern for Cáceres seem at least as powerful as those connecting people to others who live in their same nation-states.

The most important skill that citizens of the Athenian polis and the Italian city states needed to learn was the art of debate. Generally, it has been assumed that the most important skill for being a citizen of a representative democracy is the skill in being an informed voter. Many defenders of liberal democracy argue that we need to promote civil dialogue as a way to get past the anger and polarization that they see as causing present the crisis of democracy. And yet, many people move to incivility because they see governmental systems as not meeting their needs and they feel frustrated about that fact.

In "Enough of Deliberation: Politics is about Interests and Power," Ian Shapiro argues that "recent calls to inject substantial doses of deliberation into democratic politics rest on a misdiagnosis of its infirmities."[25]

> The most pressing political challenges in the United States do not result from lack of deliberation. Rather, they stem from the increasing subversion of democracy by powerful private interests. ... Unless and until that challenge can be addressed, debating what deliberation can add to politics is little more than a waste of time.[26]

Taking that critique of deliberation one step further, Xavier De Souza Briggs argues that "deliberation in practice can become one more tool for the best organized and informed to dominate the civic agenda while putting a legitimating mask on things."[27]

The path to a better society rests in the hard work of challenging the ways that power is increasingly concentrated in very few hands. And those challenges to power require more of us than being informed citizens who discuss in a civil manner and vote thoughtfully. In order to work to build a better world, we need to learn how to engage power and transform structures of power. Engaging in dialogue can help us to develop our views, and in organizing, it is generally a good idea to be as civil as possible. But the real work of making the world more democratic is about challenging power and holding it to account. And that often involves bold action, such as civil disobedience. We also need to learn to be organizers. We need to be adept at the real work of deciding what kinds of changes need to be made to challenge power, and we need to be able to mobilize those forces to make those changes. Citizenship for accountability democracy requires a temperament that is not passively fulfilling the role one has been given by dominant social forces: it also requires bravery.

In *Post-Democracy*, Colin Crouch worries that this broader notion of citizenship as related to activism may eclipse the narrower one that is anchored in the politics of the state. He makes the observation that electoral democracy is increasingly weak because of its relationship to money. He then wonders if perhaps the future of democracy lies elsewhere, in the broader notion of citizenship we have been discussing.

> Different evidence to contest my claims that democracy is weakening comes from the lively world of causes and pressure groups, which are growing in importance. Do these not constitute the embodiment of a healthy positive citizenship? There is a danger that one might concentrate too much on politics in the narrow sense of party and electoral struggle, and ignore the displacement of creative citizenship away from this arena to the wider one of cause groups.... [T]he range of objects of action available becomes far more extensive than just helping politicians get elected. And modern means of communication, like the Internet make it ever easier and cheaper to organize and co-ordinate new cause groups.[28]

And yet, he worries that replacing a citizenship that focuses on impacting the state with one that focuses on cause groups will lead to a total disengagement with the state, which will then leave that terrain, where important decisions are made, to corporations to control completely. "To desert party for cause group is only to conspire further in the triumph of post-democracy."[29]

Some anarchists, such as John Holloway in his *Change the World without Taking Power (the Meaning of Revolution Today)*, have argued that the state is so inherently corrupt as an institution, the way to a liberatory politics is through building alternative institutions and sidestepping the state entirely.[30] And yet, given that much political power is concentrated in national governments, it would be a poor idea to abandon the state as a site of struggle. Worse states are worse for the world than better states. And, the question of how we hold power to account is just as relevant for those alternative institutions as it is for a traditional state. Most accountability seeking organizations, or what Crouch calls "cause groups," see their work as in a dynamic relationship with the state.

Conclusion

The responsible citizen develops her civic virtue by being educated about the nature of the realities she faces, is well educated about real dynamics of power, is motivated by a civic sense of the importance of pursuing the common good, and is brave enough to disrupt illegitimate operations of power. The good citizen sees her obligations as related to the broad social fabric she inhabits, and not merely as relating to the nation-state she lives in, while also being a responsible citizen of that state. She uses the abilities she has to make a difference where she can.

Understanding politics narrowly as the art of government of a national territory will make politics increasingly irrelevant to the crises of accountability we are facing. Just as our concepts of morality need expand, so also must our concepts of politics be expanded to deal with a wide array of large scale, contested, slippery, and elusive powers.

Institutions and practices need to be developed that monitor, constrain, and hold to account the real configurations of power that impact our lives, the sustainability of our atmosphere, and of non-human nature. The political concepts we use must understand power in a very broad way, and must find ways to hold those powers to account. Accountability democracy engages with the wide array of powers that cause damage in the world. It operates in a decentralized way through the proliferation of accountability mechanisms.

Before delving into the theory of accountability democracy, and the accountability mechanisms through which it operates, in Chapter 6, Chapter 5 clarifies the nature of the configurations of power that are responsible for the present crisis of accountability.

5

The Destructive Powers That Need to be Held to Account

...

I don't like the idea of power. It seems so harsh. I don't think anyone should have power.[1]

That is so annoyingly liberal. You think you don't like power because all kinds of power are working to make you comfortable and you don't have to notice what they are doing in your name. Once we take state power, we will be able to use that power for the good of all. The reason things are so messed up now is that the people with power are the people who profit from the systems of domination.

I wouldn't want to see what you'd do if you had power. Power needs to be in the hands of those who can use it responsibly and who have earned that right.

You really have no idea how powerful you are. Your desires for goods are what make those good be produced in the factories

of the Global South. And your desire for them to be cheap is what makes them be produced cheaply. Your innocent fear Black people causes the police to lock them up and clean them from your neighborhood.

I think about the ways my desires and feelings hurt other people. I think about it all the time. Sometimes when I see a Black person on the street, I feel afraid. And I know it isn't right. And I know it probably hurts that person if they notice. I try really hard to not do that. But it is deep inside me. It makes me feel so bad. But I don't have the power to change that. Do I?

You can't get all political about how people feel. It's what people do that matters. As long as they don't hurt anyone, they can feel what they feel.

...

Esaw Garner's husband Eric was a father and grandfather. A large and genial man, Garner was known in his Staten Island New York as a peacemaker. He was the guy who would talk to people who were having conflicts and break up fights. He'd had to leave his job as a gardener for the New York City Department of Parks and Recreation because of ill health. Finding it difficult to make a living, Garner took to selling individual cigarettes to bring in some cash.

Garner was well known to the NYPD. Years before the incident that cost him his life, Garner had filed a complaint with the NYPD for doing a body cavity search in public. On the day he was killed, Garner was breaking up a fight, which attracted the interest of the police.

Police questioned him and when he asked why he was being questioned they responded aggressively. That was when Officer Daniel Pantaleo put

Garner into the illegal chokehold that ended his life. Garner repeated his famous last words eleven times: "I can't breathe." Rather than attending to his medical needs, officers emptied his pockets. Eight officers were standing around looking at him as he died.

...

Power

Power is the ability to get things done and to make things happen; it is effectivity and is not necessarily harmful. The desire to change the world is a desire for power. People working for social justice are looking for the ability to make things happen that they see as in the interests of those who have been subjected to domination. If we think of the goal of social justice as eliminating power, then we will be skeptical of the things that need to be done to create legitimate systems of power and legitimate ways to hold that power to account. Understanding power to mean simply domination, underlies the mistake often made by people working for social justice that once a system of domination is overthrown, the problem they address will be solved.

Not taking seriously the ways that those working for social justice need to wield power to challenge unaccountable power allows them to be surprised when revolutions for social justice put people in power who then become tyrants. Attempts to challenge power themselves use power, and well-intentioned operations of power must be held to account as much as any other operation of power. Social justice organizations usually need unions, and unions need watchdog organizations to make sure they serve the interests of their members, or in the case of racial exclusion, to make sure they serve the need of those who should be members.

According to Martin Luther King Jr., power is "the ability to achieve purpose." The morality of power has to do with what purposes it is used to achieve. Power is dangerous because it tends to accumulate. Having the ability to achieve a purpose allows an agent to transform the social landscape, which can lead to them being able to achieve more power. That snowball effect is the insight behind Gianfranco Poggi's claim that social power is "the ability to make a difference to the making of differences."[2]

In his book, *Where Do We Go from Here: Chaos or Community*, King wrote of the importance of those seeking justice to not be afraid of power.

> Power, properly understood, is the ability to achieve purpose. It is the strength required to bring about social, political, or economic changes. In this sense power is not only desirable but necessary in order to implement the demands of love and justice. One of the greatest problems of history is that the concepts of love and power are usually contrasted as polar opposites. Love is identified with a resignation of power and power with a denial of love. What is needed is a realization that power without love is reckless and abusive and that love without power is sentimental and anemic. Power at its best is love implementing the demands of justice. Justice at its best is power correcting everything that stands against love.[3]

If power is "the ability to achieve purpose" then those seeking justice need not avoid power. Instead, they need to find ways to use the powers that they have in order to keep power from accumulating in ways that are harmful. And we need to look carefully at the variety of ways that power operates.

In *The History of Sexuality*, Michel Foucault writes that

> power must be understood in the first instance as the multiplicity of force relations immanent in the sphere in which they operate and which constitute their own organization; as the process which,

through ceaseless struggles and confrontations, transforms, strengthens, or reverses them; as the support which these force relations find in one another, thus forming a chain or a system, or on the contrary, the disjunctions and contradictions which isolate them from one another; and lastly as the strategies in which they take effect, whose general design or institutional crystallization is embodied in the state apparatus, in the formulation of the law, in the various social hegemonies . . . .There is no power that is exercised without a series of aims and objectives. But this does not mean that it results from the choice or decision of an individual subject.[4]

For Foucault, power emerges from complex, historically developed discourses, which are both systems of meaning and arrangements of social institutions. Power is mobilized as a result of these discourses, and while agents, or those complex entities which wield power, come to make things happen, these agents are complex and not necessarily as simple as individuals who want to make things happen.

To give one simple example, Exxon-Mobil is presently doing all it can to burn as much fossil fuel as it can. That is because it is a corporation operating under the logic of profit maximization. Any individual CEO of Exxon-Mobil would find it very difficult to make that behemoth serve a different set of purposes. If he tried, he would be expelled before the institution changed. Changing that institution requires transforming the legal, social, and market context in which that corporation operates. The corporation comes to have a form of agency that goes beyond any individual working there.

An entity, like Exxon-Mobil, comes to accumulate power by transforming the landscape in which it operates to increase its effectivity. The millions of dollars the company spent trying to sow confusion about the climate crisis was intended to allow it to shape the context in which it operates to allow it to accumulate even more profit. Large-scale operations of power, such as transnational corporations and transnational institutions, such as the World Bank, are similar in that both operate at such a large scale that they create crises in accountability through their ability to transform governments and make them into agents of their interests.

These transnational actors differ in that multinational corporations are fundamentally driven by the pursuit of profit for their shareholders. Transnational entities, such as the World Bank, are constituted by more complex and more contested networks of agency. The World Bank is accountable to the governments that are its more powerful members, and to the complex relations of power that are expressed in the actions of those governments; and their actions are shaped by a need for legitimation; and their agency is importantly shaped by their relations to the transnational banking industry. They carry out their own operations of power through how they choose to give loans, imposing particular governmental regulations on low-income countries through the terms of those loans, and influencing transnational trade regimes.

Transnational corporations and transnational pro-capitalist institutions create a crisis of accountability by de-territorializing power.[5] Power comes to transcend local boundaries. And these institutions undermine and evade the accountability mechanisms which live in national governments and shape those governments to serve their needs. As Jessica Matthews put it,

> National Governments . . . are sharing powers—including political, social, and security roles at the core of sovereignty—with businesses, with international organizations, and with a multitude of citizens groups . . . . The steady concentration of power in the hands of states that began in 1648 with the Peace of Westphalia is over, at least for a while.[6]

According to Jeffrey Hart and Aseem Prakash,

> Post-Westphalian governance structures will reflect permeable borders, multiple and perhaps conflicting allegiances, and co-existing levels of authority—transnational, national, and sub-national. It will be a relationally rather than a hierarchically structured world in which the meaning of internal and external sovereignty becomes increasingly ambiguous.[7]

For the past several hundred years, power was in important ways constrained, produced, and deployed by social relations anchored in national governments. And as democracy has spread, the idea spread that power would be held to account by governments which were legitimized on the basis of their being accountable to their citizens. That idealized view of democratic government was never fully realized, as the powers constituted by other configurations of power have always been wrapped up in the ways that governments work.

From the beginning of the period of national governments, there have been large-scale transnational forces, such as the British East India Company, and the armed forces of colonial powers, which have been shaping and undermining the accountability mechanisms that might have existed in national governments. The slippery working of markets has increased as a way that power accumulates since that time. And the elusive operations of system of meaning, have always been there influencing the operations of national governments. Also, always at play, since the beginning of the period of national governments, have been the realities of wealth disparities, and the impact of money on government, as well as the limitations which have existed on citizenship. National governments are always contested sites, where power is concentrated, contested, and deployed. They are never fully accountable, neutral containers of power.

Nation-states accumulate and disperse power through a variety of mechanisms. States are able to mobilize violence and use it against their citizens, as well as against other states. States are able to set rules that must be followed by individual citizens, and they can enforce those rules through violence. States raise taxes and deploy the resources embodied in those monies to carry out a myriad of projects. Which interests a government serves is the result of a constant tug of war among a wide variety of forces.

The slippery power of markets is also shaped by a variety of practices. There are the laws that shape trade deals and construct what can be sold where for what price. There are the regulations which allow some practices and forbid others. There is the ideology that says that once something is perceived as operating according to a market it becomes resistant to intentional intervention, because those regulations "distort" the workings of the market. That idea then pushes moral judgment out of huge swaths of social life, as the "market decides" where housing will be built, how much workers are paid, and who gets medical care. Markets are always regulated and being reregulated. But the spread of the myth that markets must be allowed the freedom to work their magic is one of the most powerful elements in pro-capitalist thinking. And when that way of thinking is widespread, when the system of regulations under which a market operates are allowed to wreak havoc on people lives, and when morality is thrown out of the system, we have a crisis of accountability.

Once a market is established in a particular way, chains of decisions lead to things being made, resources being pulled out of the Earth, labor being mobilized and deployed, workers whose bodies have been destroyed being tossed aside, objects being moved, and consumer needs being created and satisfied, all with immunity from responsibility for actors all along that chain. This market immunity made Rana Plaza collapse. And that is why markets are called a slippery configuration of power. A market is social effectivity which slips past the grip of explicit responsibility for anyone or anything in particular for its impacts. Markets create a crisis of accountability by embedding power in a configuration which evades our ability to assert human and ecological needs over how society operates.

Finally, systems of meaning mobilize social passions to encourage people to vote certain ways, to treat others in certain ways, to spend money in certain ways, and to care about some things and not others. Belief in the dispassionate efficiency of markets allows them to run rampant over people's lives and to not be constrained in ways that protect people's livelihoods. Commercial interests can pay for media to shape how we understand the world in ways that serve those interests. There are always forces at work, large and small, which shape how we understand the world. The Italian philosopher Antonio Gramsci called the ways that power comes to be embedded in a system of meaning hegemony, and he argued that an important part of work for justice was to create counter-hegemonies, or ways of understanding and experiencing the world which would diffuse and disrupt the ways that systems of meaning concentrate dominating operations of power.[8]

This configuration of power is elusive, because it is hard to see the fingerprints of the intentions of any particular agents in mobilizing its resources. Systems of meaning create a crisis of accountability through the ways that they allow social resources to be mobilized and deployed without it being easy to nail down where the problem is coming from, who to hold responsible, or how to hold them responsible.

The way out of the present crisis of accountability is to expose and understand these operations of power and to develop and strengthen mechanisms to hold them to account. Contrasting theories of accountability with the Marxist goal of eliminating power, Andreas Schedler argues that the guiding idea of political accountability is to control political power, not to eliminate it. In this sense, political accountability presupposes power. Far from harboring utopias of power disappearing, withering away, the notion of political accountability enters a world of power . . . .[9] [Accountability] is a more modest project that admits that politics is a human enterprise whose elements of agency, freedom, indeterminacy, and uncertainty are ineradicable; that power cannot be subject to full control in the strict technical sense of the word.[10]

Schedler, like many theorists of accountability, bases his work on a humble, and very helpful, approach to power. These theorists of accountability focus on ways to control the inevitable ways that power tends to accumulate and can be used in socially negative ways. Rather than focusing on simply challenging injustices, theorists of accountability focus on how to build systems that prevent abuse. This is based on a theory of power that holds that whenever there are inequalities of power, there is a potential for those with power to abuse it, and that it is inevitable that inequalities of power will emerge and need to be reined in. The question for politics then becomes how to set up processes that will constantly monitor the ways that power accumulates, ways to disperse unjust accumulations of power, and ways to hold those with power to account, such that those accumulations of power are limited.

Agency and Power: The Nature of Social Formations

Power—or the ability to make things happen—is embedded in complex social systems that evolve over time. Michael Omi and Howard Winant develop the concept *racial formation*, in their book

Racial Formation in the United States from the 1960s to the 1990s, to explain how the system of racism evolved over time. I use their way of understanding the relationship between structure and agency and extend it to talk about social formations in general.

They argue that racial formations evolve as the results of the actions of a variety of forms of agency over time. Racial formations begin in projects that some people have, but evolve and take on lives of their own, and become forms of agency in themselves.

As Columbus's original plan to open a trade route to India didn't work out and he tried to find another way to profit from his adventures, the systems of slavery and colonialism began to form. Racism was not an original intent of that project, but quickly grew out of it.

> The "discovery" signaled a break from previous proto-racial awareness by which Europe contemplated its "others" in a relatively disorganized fashion. The "conquest of America" was not simply an epochal historical event—however unparalleled in importance. It was also the advent of a consolidated social structure of exploitation, appropriation, domination, and signification. Its representation, first in religious terms, later in scientific and political ones, initiated modern racial awareness. It was the inauguration of racialization on a world-historical scale.[11]

Racism began with one set of intentions of one group of people and over time metamorphosed into a system of power that is deeply embedded in the fabric of many of the world's societies. Omi and Winant use the concept "racial project" to describe the forms of agency that grow around the embedding in the social fabric over time, of practices that have to do with what has come to be racism.

Extending this concept to cover social processes in general, we can say that agents are formed by social processes and those social processes also form agents. Power comes to be embedded in these social processes in complex ways. Some of these forms of agency have to do with law, and are anchored in governments, and transnational legal apparatuses; others are anchored in systems of meaning, and norms; some are anchored in our bodies and the things we desire; others are anchored in how we understand the nature of those social systems we live in. Foucault uses the word "discourse" to describe these complex configurations of power and agency.

Making the case that power works through systems of meaning as much as it does through economic and legal systems, Stuart Hall argues that

> how things are represented and the "machineries" and regimes of representation in a culture do play a *constitutive*, and not merely a reflexive, after-the-event, role. This gives questions of culture and ideology, and the scenarios of representation—subjectivity, identity, politics—a formative, not merely expressive, place in the constitution of social and political life.[12]

Thus, a social formation includes material as well as ideal aspects. It is anchored in a wide array of processes, which include systems of meaning, control over resources, control over violence, as well as ways that we experience our own bodies.

Power in Government

The ideal of representative government is based on the belief that by electing people to decide on laws and on the allocation of resources and by granting administrative bureaucracies the ability to carry out those decisions, power within a national territory will be held to account. And yet, states are never neutral containers of power. Rather, they are places where battles over power are fought out.

And power is always at the heart of what is being negotiated in government. According to Ian Shapiro,

> Political institutions differ from other sites of collective human activity in that the exercise of power is not incidental to the pursuit of some further goal; it is integral to the nature of the beast.[13]

He argues that a democratic system of government should be judged on the basis of "how well it enables people to manage power relations as judged by the yardstick of minimizing domination."[14]

Much of what has been written on accountability focuses on ways to make government actions accountable and to hold companies accountable to certain regulations and tax laws that are anchored in those national governments. Many governments have accountability mechanisms to ensure that legislators or administrators of governmental bureaucracies are not taking bribes, or giving special favors to family members.

And yet the power that comes to be concentrated in governments operates in damaging ways that those accountability mechanisms were not designed to catch. The killing of Eric Garner by Daniel Pantaleo of the NYPD was not an anomaly. Rather, it was part of a deep and persistent pattern that grew out of the history of policing in the United States being used to maintain the boundaries of the country's racial order. If a jury believes that a police officer had reason to fear for their lives, then the law protecting people from being killed for no reason don't apply. The rule of law is too malleable to be enough to stop police murder in a society where the dehumanization of Black people is a widespread, shared understanding.

Representative governments can be seen as places where different social forces vie for control, and where sometimes, as with the legislation that followed the civil rights movement, that apparatus can be made to operate in the interest of an equal distribution of power.

And we can see with the war on drugs, how the concessions given to the civil rights movement were followed by a whole different strategy for disenfranchizing people of color through mass incarceration, and thus a re-concentration of power among whites.

Governments hold tremendous resources to make things happen and to prevent other things from happening. The forms of agency which become embedded in their operations grow out of struggles over long periods of time. In the United States, governmental power is distorted in important ways by the racial dynamics of white supremacy to this day.

Ever since the election of Trump, I have found myself appreciating the rule of law in ways that I never had before. As a leftist, I have generally been suspicious of the ways that modern states use the power that is concentrated in them for unjust forms of policing; to control and manage society in the interests of pro-capitalist policies; and in the United States to manage the largest military operation in world history, which is mostly used to keep the world safe for transnational capital.

After that election, it became clearer to many of us, that if some people are going to control the amount of power that is accumulated in a modern state, such as military and police forces, then the power vested in that state needs to be as accountable as possible. And laws which are supposed to be neutral and fair are not a bad thing to fight for. It is not enough to say that states are unjust because they control apparatuses of violence and are generally controlled by those with power. Those of us wanting a socially just diffusion of power need to also attend to the ways that power accumulates in states and we need to work to hold those configurations of power to account.

Thinkers on the left, whether Marxist or Anarchist, have tended not to give much attention to the question of how to hold the power that is concentrated in governments to account. For

Marxists, the state under capitalism is generally seen as a bourgeois state that exists to support a capitalist economy. Marxists, such as Lenin, have hoped that once that bourgeois state was overthrown, a government that represented popular interest would come into being. Lacking any system of rule of law and checks and balances on power, most states that have called themselves Marxist have had governments that were abusive, and which allowed horrific accumulations of power to rest in the hands of those controlling the state, and in the police apparatuses that worked as agents of the state.

More sophisticated Marxist analysts of the state, such Nicos Poulantzas, have argued that the state is a site of contestation and that it is more than an apparatus to be use by the bourgeoisie under capitalism or the working class under socialism. And yet even Poulantzas, does not develop a theory of how to keep the power invested in a state accountable to its citizens.

To this day there is very little work done among Marxists to develop ideas for how to keep the power that is accumulated in a state from being used in unjust ways. Contemporary Marxists tend to scoff at notions of the rule of law as bourgeois niceties, and to suppose that the authoritarian states that ruled in the name of Marxism were taken over by corrupt individuals.

Anarchists tend to define the state as that entity which has a monopoly of violence within a given territory. For them, the state is defined as a system of legitimized force. Because they believe in autonomy, they tend to oppose government completely. Anarchist theory is full of descriptions of how to organize in ways that foster engagement and participation. But they have little to say about how to set up large-scale social structures, which is one definition of the state, which will allow for complex social interaction and yet will keep power from accumulating in unaccountable ways.

Marxism and Anarchism share a belief that the goal of human development should be a world without governments that use force to control people. Neither tradition has done as much as it could to help us understand how to engage with the powers that are concentrated in states in the present moment.

For as long as we have governments, it is important that governmental power be as accountable as possible. Systems of law are sites of contestation where laws can sometimes be passed that hold power to account. Governments need to be constantly monitored and challenged such that laws that embed and enable unequal configurations of power need to be constantly challenged. Because of the power of money in elections, and the power embedded in the systems of meaning that any government is embedded in, we need to always understand that systems of law are not neutral. The state is an apparatus for the concentration and dispersal of power in a particular territory. Governmental action is always the result of a history of contests over who will control each aspect of that apparatus of power. The ideal of national governments as neutral containers for power is largely illusory.[15]

There have been times in US history when popular interests were more ascendant and where the representatives acting in the public interest have been able to enact policies that diffuse power and hold it to account. In the United States, right now we are in a period where the elected officials are to a large extent representing the interests of the 1%. And the 1% is busily rewriting the rules of the game to further ensure their continued ability to enable extreme operations of power.

Holding a representative government accountable involves more than the transparency and anti-corruption measures called for by traditional advocates of accountability. It would involve taking the insidious power of money out of the system. It would involve ensuring that race and gender prejudice were not able to distort the rule of law. It would involve practices of democracy that engaged people such that they felt that the decisions made by a government were something that they could impact, and that there was a fair process where solutions could be generated to the challenges we all face of how to live together well.

Large-Scale Operations of Power

Entities such as transnational corporations and transnational pro-corporate institutions such as the International Monetary Fund operate at such a large scale that national governments, even when they try to limit their behavior, are constrained in their ability to hold them to account. If a company such as Exxon-Mobil doesn't like the conditions imposed on it by one government, it can move operations to another. It can pour so much money into an election that it can pressure governments to act in their interest. And it can influence the rules of the transnational trading system such that it can find favorable conditions for its operations in many locations.

Transnational corporations have huge amounts of power embedded in them. That power exists in the money they can spend to influence governments, in the control they have over shaping markets, and in their ability to advertise and hook us into the systems of desire they stimulate through the advertising that feeds their profits.

The powers of transnational structures such as the World Trade Organization, the International Monetary Fund, and the European Union have tremendous impact on our lives and we have very little direct ability to control them. A functioning system of accountability needs to be able to challenge these large-scale operations of power.

The Transpacific Partnership (TPP) was a deeply pro-corporate trade agreement that was being negotiated between twelve countries until Trump was elected and pulled the United States out of the process. For the countries that stayed in a renamed version of that agreement, it has made the terms of trade between those countries increasingly operate in the interests of multinational corporations. Those corporations, and the institutions that support them, are working hard to use the powers they have to get governments to set rules that increase their ability to make profits.

Such trade agreements create new forms of agency as they push nations to have regulations that will favor big capital over small-scale local producers, and over environmental and human rights regulations. Small producers get thrown out of business by "the market" but the market is not a neutral force. It will have been shaped through the agency of these larger forces. And when popular opposition to these agreements causes them to fail, the people can be said to have exerted a democratizing influence on the market.

The global network of tax havens has tremendous power to suck resources from people all around the world and concentrate them in the hands of a small global elite. That global elite then uses the power that is embodied in money (which Marx saw as congealed social power) to make all sorts of things happen, from buying governments and undermining regulations to burning absurd amounts of fossil fuels in their pursuit of entertainment. Those tax havens exist as a result of tremendous cooperative work among global elites who act to create conditions for their own accumulation of the power embedded in money. We are in a period where the power of people over their governments is waning, as the power of finance capital is increasingly unconstrained and is supported and enabled by national governments or transnational organizations.

Power in Systems of Meaning

If Eric Garner had been killed five years earlier, his murder would likely have received no media attention and no one would have been held to account. As a result of the movement to challenge police violence, there is a shift taking place in US society toward accountability for how legal systems treat Black people. The hashtag #BlackLivesMatter, launched after the murder of Trayvon Martin, helped transform the routine killing of Black people by the police and vigilantes into something seen widely as an outrage against their humanity.[16] The protests that took place after the murder of Michael Brown in Ferguson amplified that moral outrage. Legal systems began to prosecute those killings more than that had been done in the past. The movement then tried to have jail time imposed on the murderers as a sanction for those wrongs.

One of the hardest things that the Movement for Black Lives has been up against is that Black Lives are often not seen as mattering strongly enough by people who administer the criminal justice system, and those who serve on juries. We can have rights, but if those charged with protecting our rights don't see us as fully human, then those rights will not be enforced. As Patricia Williams argues, "The problem with rights discourses is not that the discourse itself is constricting but that it exists in a constricted referential universe."[17] Having the legal system ready to protect the rights of Black people involves a transformation of deep structures of meaning that have existed for centuries, such that society as a whole will see them as deserving of rights.

The dehumanization at the root of this lack of rights is not an accident or a simple prejudice; instead, it is deeply rooted in the history of slavery. As Cheryl Harris argues,

> The hyper-exploitation of Black labor was accomplished by treating Black people themselves as objects of property. Race and property were thus conflated by establishing a form of property contingent on race—only Blacks were subjugated as slaves and treated as property.[18]

For hundreds of years, human beings were defined in the United States as white people, and having property was seen as an important marker of humanity. Black people were seen not as owners of property but instead as themselves being property. Sylvia Wynter sees this as part of the set of social processes unleashed 500 years ago with the origins of capitalism.

She argues that

> the large-scale accumulation of unpaid land, unpaid labor, and overall wealth expropriated by Western Europe from non-European peoples, which was to lay the basis of its global expansion from the fifteenth century onwards, was carried out within the order of truth and the self-evident order of consciousness, of a creed-specific conception of what it was to be human.[19]

Wynter argues that many forms of oppression are based on a concept of Man as a property-owning, autonomous, and rational male, who is seen as an agent and a bearer of rights in a world of things and other people taken to be objects of exploitation.

> In the context of the secular human, black subjects, along with indigenous populations, the colonized, the insane, the poor, the disabled, and so on, serve as limit cases by which Man can demarcate himself as the universal human.[20]

Alexander Weheliye develops Wynters's ideas and claims that "blackness designates a changing system of unequal power structures that apportion and limit which humans can lay claim to full human status and which humans cannot."[21] The deep systems of relations that are anchored in that history of dehumanization resonate through our political and social systems in ways that are routinely painful, and sometimes lethal, for those constructed in ways that deny their full humanity. Holding to account the power that causes that pain, and sometimes death, will involve a deep transformation of the systems of meaning that deny the full rights of citizenship to Black people.

This is why the voice and value aspects of the accountability mechanisms that are developing to challenge police murder have been so important. And it also explains how hard it is to gain enough power to make sanctions stick against violators of those rights.

When we look at the configuration of power that allowed Eric Garner to be murdered, and his murderer to keep working for the NYPD for many years, we see a supposedly neutral legal system that is deeply distorted by the dehumanization of a large part of the US population. There are laws in the United States that prevent people from killing unarmed civilians, and generally people who do so go to jail if they are caught. And yet, in the United States, police officers have for many years had the power to kill unarmed Black people with impunity.

The crucial difference with the police killings of people of color is that those lives haven't been valued in the dominant US culture. That system of meaning is grounded in the entrenched legacy of racism, which causes harm in ways that are often invisible, and often without anyone breaking any laws or doing anything they are told is morally unacceptable. And it allows for the laws to be ignored when the actions fit with the sense of meaning of the dominant majority.

The movement to challenge police impunity has been given focus and strength by the slogan "Black Lives Matter." That slogan has been so politically productive because it names something that has been true for a long time: that the police are able to kill without consequences because the society as a whole doesn't value Black lives. The slogan, and the visibility of the killings that have come since the slogan, have led to hope for a transformation of the ways the legal system responds to that class of murders.

The power that exists in the dehumanization of Black people is not just a shallow set of ideas that can be destroyed by arguing against them. Instead, those systems of meaning come to live deeply within our bodies. Foucault used the term "bio-power" to describe the sort of power that actually creates our sense of self and that helps construct our desires. In *Discipline and Punish*, he describes the way the human body was disciplined in the early days of the factory system to prepare workers to be able to sit still and take orders for hours every day. That disciplining takes years of training, and it is, he argues, one of the main accomplishments of public-school systems: to ready our bodies for wage labor. That process of disciplining is the internalization of dominant systems of power into our bodies.[22]

Deleuze and Guatari use the term "capitalist-desiring subjects" to describe the ways that capitalist ways of constructing meaning come to influence what we want and to turn us into agents of capitalist markets.[23] In a capitalist society, that desire becomes one of the most prized targets of the marketer's craft.

In *The Art of Loving*, Eric Fromm discusses the ways that capitalist culture colonizes our deepest desires, including what makes us fall in love.

> Modern man's [sic] happiness consists of the thrill of looking at the shop windows, and in buying all that he can afford to buy. . . . "Attractive" usually means a nice package of qualities which are popular and sought after on the personality market. What specifically makes a person attractive depends on the fashion of the time, physically as well as mentally.[24]

The elusive configurations of power that are embedded in systems of meaning and desire are not insignificant. They supply much of the energy that can be used and manipulated for governmental power, as in laws that make gender non-conforming behavior illegal. In the case of the assault on Black and Brown people by the police, the elusive power embedded in people's felt reality comes to be given lethal power when the government enables some people to react to those feelings with guns and prisons. Systems of desire, such as consumer culture, have been propagated because they are in the interests of those seeking to profit off of our purchases, even though it is clear that following the dictates of consumer culture doesn't lead to happiness.[25]

One powerful way to challenge the power concentrated in toxic systems of meaning is to develop alternative systems of meaning, or what Gramsci called counter-hegemonies. The development of counter-hegemonies is an important early part of any social movement. In the United States, the queer liberation movement has challenged heteronormative ways and encouraged the whole culture to be more relaxed about sexual and gender norms. Those cultural changes have been an important part of the move toward significant changes in laws.[26]

People from an older generation, who grew up with strongly homophobic and heteronormative values, experience those antipathies as if they were a deep part of themselves. And yet younger people in the United States increasingly don't understand why gender rules are even an issue. They have developed as human beings in a period in which counter-hegemonic ways of experiencing sexuality and gender have circulated widely, and in which the older homophobic and transphobic ways of understanding their own sexuality were not pushed on them as deeply.

Accountability mechanisms that develop to deal with the elusive configurations of power embedded in systems of meaning will involve democratizing the means of influencing culture and calling out attempts to mobilize desires for the purposes of domination. It will require social movements that create counter-hegemonies and transform how we understand the humanity of people from marginalized groups, and how we feel about ourselves and others. It will also involve challenging the misuses of governmental power that grow out of mobilizing the hatreds of people from specific groups to gain other forms of power.

The Power of the Market

...

I am the magical invisible hand. See my beautiful long fingers and their sweep as I flip my wrist and make all of your dreams come true. You want a beautiful house with three bathrooms? Poof and viola, and here it is. Oh, you'd rather it have granite countertops? Poof and voila, very nice. I have infinite powers; I am a dreamweaver. I live to make dreams come true. Any desire, bring it to me and I will fulfill it. Everything I do is done in the best way possible. I move things around from place to place and make everyone who can use my magic be as happy as they can be. How do I do it? Money of course is the lifeblood of my magic. Where does the money come from and who does the labor to make the things I give out so efficiently? Please don't make me answer those questions. Oh, and please don't mind those trolls laboring away in the dungeon.

...

The ideal of the free market says that things should sell for their natural price, and prices should be set by the unseen working of the invisible hand of the market. Capitalist markets are said to work best without intentional decisions being made by anyone. This means that no one is to be held responsible for the low wages being paid by the garment industry in Bangladesh. No one is responsible for the decision of consumers to drive cars, or to sell food that travels thousands of miles before getting to our plates.

The set of ideas that underlie the idea of the market as autonomous and neutral was promoted by many different thinkers over a long period of time. John Locke was one of its early promoters, with his idea that we can understand social relationships by imagining ourselves in a state of nature where we are all free and autonomous. The market, on this idea, is a set of free interactions that individuals engage in to get what they need. Adam Smith is often used as a founding figure in this set of ideas, but in fact he argued that markets needed to be embedded in governmental systems that would ensure moral outcomes.[27]

In his 1944 classic text, *The Great Transformation*, Karl Polanyi argued that human societies have had markets for thousands of years. Those older markets were embedded in systems of social relations that made the market subordinate to other social forces. In many human societies, over the millennia, people have worked the land they live on, and that land has been controlled by social agreements that were sometimes more, and sometimes less democratic.[28]

People have generally made most of what they needed to survive. And for millennia, people have used markets to trade some goods with one another. Those markets have had rules that guide how they work, and most of what people need to survive has not been attained through a market process. Polanyi argued that what was world changing about the development of the capitalist market, as it emerged over the past few hundred years, is that there came to be markets in things that newly came to be seen as commodities to be traded: land, labor, and money. In previous times land and labor were allocated by other complex social mechanisms, and money did not exist in its modern form. The capitalist market is created by the beliefs, and institutional processes to back them, that create markets in land, labor, and money, and which argue that trade should happen with as little influence from other social processes as possible.

In *The Power of Market Fundamentalism: Karl Polanyi's Critique,* Fred Block and Margaret Sommers argue that markets are always being regulated and enabled in a variety of ways. Some regulations make it such that investors can be sure governments will go after those who don't pay their bills, and some regulations such as the dispute mechanisms in the World Trade Organization make it such that governments are limited in their ability to impose environmental regulations on corporations. The regulations through which markets are created are sometimes in the interests of people and the environment, and they are sometimes enacted in the interests of those seeking increased profits.[29] There has never been an unregulated market.

The myth of the "free market" hides those practices of regulation, and makes it difficult for those wanting to regulate a market in the interest of holding capital to account. I have been involved with several struggles to enact rent control. It is inevitable what when speaking on the issue in public, at least one opponent will say that what we are proposing is absurd because Economics 101 teaches us that if you mess with the market you will get perverse outcomes. They claim that regulating rents will lead to there being less housing. And yet the market is already not providing enough housing for low-income people, including in places where there is no rent control, because there is little profit to be made in the lower end of the housing market.

Almost every introductory economics class taught in the United States, and many of those taught in other countries, preaches this same gospel. And the ideals taught there are fairly widespread. This set of beliefs has helped protect pro-capitalist interests from having to take responsibility for the negative impacts of economic policies that favor the wealthy.[30]

Systems of power come to be developed that end up hiding the fingerprints of those battles over economic policy, such that the working of the market come to appear as normal and natural and not anyone's responsibility. The market hides power by setting up an ideology that claims assertively that markets are natural and not to be interfered with, and that no one should be held responsible for their operations. Once they are set up, markets become an important form of agency for the reproduction of capitalism. When I buy clothing based on the best value I can get for the price, I am allowing the market to decide who makes my clothes and under what circumstances.

Holding markets accountable involves making visible the work that is done to shape the market; exposing the work that is done in Economics classes to make that shaping invisible; and holding to account those actors who shape markets in ways that are harmful to people and the planet. Until we do this, markets will have the slippery quality of impacting people's lives while dispersing power along endless chains of interactions that encourage unaccountable behavior among economic actors.

Holding to Account the Power of Those Who Challenge Power

When I was in graduate school, I was part of a successful effort to unionize the teaching assistants. At one point we sent a team in to negotiate our first contract with the administration. There was a lot of concern that the negotiators, who had the power to speak for us, would end up feeling pressure to be congenial in their connection with the power holders they were confronting, and would achieve the purposes of the administration as much as they achieved the purposes of the membership as a whole. We formed affinity groups and had over 100 members sit on the lawn outside the building where the negotiations were taking place. The negotiators brought out proposals to us, and we deliberated over them. We had one spokesperson from each circle form a circle of representatives. Then deliberated again, and finally sent a message along to the negotiating team about our opinion on the contract language being agreed to. This process led to a healthy, if complex and time consuming, process of accountability, and we ended up with a contract that our members were happy with.

The process of organizing through affinity groups and spokes councils is one way that people in social justice movements keep each other accountable for their actions as a group. This is an especially powerful practice for when a group of people is intending to engage in some sort of high-risk behavior, such as civil disobedience, or high-stakes action such as negotiating a contract.

Wherever there is power, or the ability to achieve purpose, there will be people with different purposes, and there will be a tendency for those in a position to make a difference to not act in the interest of everyone concerned. The left has seen this problem most acutely when revolutions have brought left-wing leaders to power in government. At the present stage of history, no one should be surprised when a group of well-meaning individuals comes to power through a revolution, that at some point a small group will end up in power and will use that power for domination.

In *State, Power, Socialism*, Polantzas argues against Marxists who suppose that because modern states are generally dominated by the capitalist class, what is required for liberation is a dual power, or a new state to emerge that has none of the institutions of the old one. He argues that parliamentary democracy is necessary for a liberated state, and that the way to get there is through what Gramsci calls a "war of position."[31] By building counterpowers to the power of capital over the state, people representing the interests of the working class can challenge the ways that the state functions to serve the interests of capital. Through a series of stepwise moves, some of which involve disruption, and some of which involve creating counter-hegemony, or a way of understanding the world that will help people to push for and vote for things in the people's interest, a state can be simultaneously challenged and transformed.

Polantzas argues against critics who say that if you come to state power through elections and a war of position, you are taking a risk that the capitalist class will continue to dominate your politics. He claims that while the Gramscian approach may not work out and the capitalists may still dominate the state, the other path, of a violent overthrow, has serious risks as well, especially when the new government does not have mechanisms built into it to limit power.

> If we weigh up the risks, that is in any case preferable to massacring other people only to end up ourselves beneath the blade of a Committee of Public Safety or some Dictator of the proletariat.[32]

Organizations that attempt to monitor power need to be monitored to ensure that they stay on the tasks they were set out to achieve and especially to ensure that money given to them ends up where it is intended to go. I am on the board of an animal welfare organization, the *Humane Farming Association*. In recent years, it has been battling with organizations that look on the surface like animal welfare organizations, but which have become little more than money making machines.

Just as the powers that we normally think of as prone to injustice, such as governments and transnational corporations, need to be monitored, so also do the powers that come from being a watchdog organization. And as accountability democracy becomes a more prevalent way of challenging power, and as monitory organizations are becoming ever more prominent parts of our political world, organizations that watch the watchers also need to become more important.

In analyzing the real-world impacts of an accountability mechanism, it is crucial that we keep the elements of real relations of power in our frame. In their article, "The Global Coalition against Corruption: Evaluating Transparency International" Fredrik Galtung and Jeremy Pope discuss the history and challenges of Transparency International (TI), a very impactful organization that fights corruption.[33] They point out that the founders of TI had worked at the World Bank and wanted to get the bank to challenge systemic forms of corruption such as bribery. The World Bank rejected this request because it was too "political."

TI came into being because the networks of power that the bank is embedded in would not allow this bolder form of action. Over time the organization has developed, and there are semi-independent chapters in countries around the world. Each chapter has its own accountability mechanism to ensure that it does not itself become a vector of corruption.[34]

For bribery to take place there need to be three elements: the one who pays the bribe, the one who takes the bribe, and the one who is cheated out of something rightly theirs, in many cases a government that deserves tax payments.[35] Most of the work of TI has been about helping governments set up systems to catch the takers of bribes, and to ensure that government process are strong enough to prevent and punish the taking of bribes.

Because of the power relations involved, it has been much easier to criticize the heads of states that are dependent on the international community for their survival for the ways that they allow bribe taking, than it has been to go after the multinational corporations that pay those bribes, or the wealthy home countries that could punish those companies for their actions.

It took a while for it to begin to do this work, but in 2006, TI published its first Bribe Payers Index, and that work has grown since.[36] With this index, the powerful payers of bribes, such as transnational corporations based in the Global North, are called out for their part in not paying taxes and fostering corrupt governments mostly in the Global South. TI has been effective not only at challenging power but also at being strategic about deciding when to take on what powers.

Conclusion

Our existing legal structures can be called on to constrain the unaccountable power of police to murder Black and Brown people. But as long as the system as a whole does not value those lives, those legal structures will have the flexibility to allow those officers to keep their jobs and not be prosecuted for murder.[37] The damaging powers we face interact with one another in complex and often unpredictable ways. The powers embedded in systems of meaning come to impact how people vote and how agents of government act. Transnational entities shape markets, which then appear to people as if they were natural, and the impacts of the market throw people out of jobs and impact who they elect.

We need to develop our understanding of the damaging powers we face, and we need to understand the leverage points that exist for taming and limiting those powers. We need to focus our attention on ways to hold the large-scale powers concentrated in transnational entities to account. We need to find accountability mechanisms that will challenge the powers imbedded in governments. We need to expose the powers that constitute markets. And we need to understand the ways that the powers embodied in the elusive nature of systems of meaning and desire can be transformed and shifted. Our analysis of what we are up against needs to be updated, as does our analysis of the most effective ways to tame, constrain, and hold to account these damaging operations of power.

6
Accountability

I'm going to try to live my life according to my values. I'm going to make every action count. I'm going to stop buying useless junk. I'm going to stop driving or eating meat. Maybe others will follow my lead. And if they don't that's their choice. I begin by holding myself to account.

Your belief in your own importance is astonishing. As if the whole world orbited around you and your goodness. The moral purity of your actions might matter to your God, but they don't change the circumstances of my life, for which you are, to some degree, responsible. The hardness of our lives comes from the centuries of slavery, the decades of colonialism, and the legacy of neocolonialism. That legacy continues. And you hold power over your government to change those circumstances.

I hate it when people play the victim. As if they had no responsibility for anything. As if everyone else was responsible for their lives. Colonialism was a long time ago. You've been on your own and now for decades, and it is time to clean up your own countries and hold your governments to account. How about starting with cleaning up the corruption? Once you stop them from fleecing the people of your country you'd be on a better path. We should help with that.

You can't understand the disasters going on in the countries of the Global South, like Guatemala, and only focus on the need to develop anti-corruption techniques. How nice to sponsor projects to clean up the water and develop a less corrupt judiciary. Is there no shame in seeing yourselves as helping those people who our government murdered, raped, and traumatized? They need to heal from the traumas we have committed on them. Their economies need to be freed from the pressures of the global finance system. Their land needs to go to the people and not be destroyed by the mining companies. They will not be able to heal the trauma and transform their economies with better bookkeeping methods. **Could it be that the focus on these small things is related to NGOs being sponsored by the World Bank; to the funders wanting results and not wanting controversy; to the discomfort with naming capitalism and other forms of institutionalized power; to people's research taking place within a matrix of control that offers them comfort, status, and success?**

So, you are saying we need to look at the big picture and see what got us into any particular mess we are looking at. I think if you look at the big picture, it is always the big players who are to blame. But good luck getting them to change.

Accountability requires action to challenge power at its deepest levels. Anything else is window-dressing.

...

When a catastrophe such as the collapse of Rana Plaza happens, many people try to find who is at fault and often get a bit uncomfortable when that fault rests with the consumers and the governments of the nations of consumers. More significant than questions such as "Who made this mess happen?" and "Who will be punished right now?" are ones about lax regulatory regimes, about anti-union activity, about support for corrupt regimes, about the impact of consumer choice, the power of boycotts, and fair-trade mechanisms.

A productive analysis of the problem needs to step back from using outdated moral concepts that look for individuals who have broken social norms, sanctions regimes that focus on those individuals, legal concepts that focus on punishment, and economic concepts that leave us with no morality at all. Instead we should focus our attention on the real fabric of the social relations that connect us, and to see the ways that that fabric can be strengthened.

Accountability democracy is built through the actions people take which create and strengthen accountability mechanisms. That important work happens at all places where unjust concentrations of power exist. This chapter looks at what goes into building effective accountability mechanisms. Accountability is a concept that is gaining increasing attention, especially in the worlds of nongovernmental organizations and governance in the Global South. In both of those areas there is serious work being done to answer the question of how to keep systems of domination from destroying people's lives, and how to build better social systems. In these literatures there are descriptions of practices that are making profound differences, and part of the effectiveness of many of them has to do with the choices people in each of these areas have made to dig into a particular set of problems and find solutions that have traction.

In the literature on accountability in the world of development nonprofits aimed at eliminating poverty, or the effects of poverty, there is a lot of attention paid to problems of corruption and mismanagement of the systems that exist, and on how to make individual projects more effective, by making them more accountable to a variety of stakeholders. And there is attention paid to how the poor could ask for their fair share of what those systems were designed to offer. But there is very little attention paid to the social processes that lead to poverty. There is virtual silence on questions of how to challenge the larger macrostructures in which these painful dramas play out. There is very little mention of global capitalism, the legacies of empire and slavery, or of the power of social movements.

In the literature on accountability in government there is a lot of attention on the systems that can be developed to fight corruption, to develop fair judicial systems, and the like. There is very little attention paid to the economic and political context in which those national governments exist.

Typically, theorists of accountability focus on two main elements: voice and sanction. An accountability mechanism exists when people who are aggrieved are able to voice their grievances, and when that voicing leads to some form of sanction. The classic case of accountability is an ombudsman. Many institutions have an office you can call if there is a problem. You voice your grievance to that office, and it is the job of that office to see that those causing the problem are alerted to the situation, and the problem is then, hopefully, stopped.

Exxon-Mobil is embedded in a few accountability mechanisms. The company is accountable to its shareholders, to maximize profits for them. It is accountable to the governments of the nations where it operates to follow the law. And the individuals who work for it are accountable to follow company policies. For each of those accountability demands, people who feel that something is wrong are in principle able to alert the right authorities, and those authorities, in principle, have the ability to sanction those causing the problem.

Missing from this picture are the systems of accountability that would challenge the company's ability to fund a climate denial industry; that challenge the influence the company has over government regulations; that challenge its use of the atmosphere as a dumping ground. In order to develop accountability for those problems, we need to expand the scope of our approach to accountability. It needs to allow a wider range of problems to be considered. It needs to have a broader notion of who to hold responsible. And it needs to attend to ways to get enough power to be effective.

For an accountability mechanism to work to challenge power, there need to be not just the two elements of voice and sanction in place. There also need to be three more elements: *values* that give meaning to something being voiced as a legitimate problem; a clear line of *responsibility* to address the sanction to someone in particular; and, finally, the *power* to make the sanction have impact. The voice needs to have meaning, the sanction needs to have a target, and the sanction needs to be enforceable.

Values

If the culture does not recognize Exxon-Mobil's funding of a climate denial industry as having violated any particular law or responsibility, then exposing it does not open the company up to being held accountable. Low-wage labor can be seen as an unfortunate side effect of the natural working of the market. Climate change can be seen as an unfortunate side effect of our need for energy. Governments acting in ways that serve the wealthy can be seen as just the way things are. When police kill innocent people, it can be understood as an unfortunate side effect of the fact that policing is a stressful job.

As long as bad things are seen as normal, unfortunate accidents, or as the cost of doing business, no amount of voicing the pains that come from them will lead to accountability. Those pains need to be framed as violations of some sort of a norm that matters, if they are to become part of an accountability mechanism that can challenge power. Part of setting up an accountability mechanism is the work of placing the pain in a value-laden framework, as meaning that something went wrong that needs to be called to account.

The work that Occupy Wall Street did in 2011 to expose and vilify the economic rule of the 1% made a significant impact on the systems of legitimation that are part of the current system of economic inequality in the United States. If people believe that the inequality we have is acceptable, then they are not likely to want to regulate the banks. If they see the foreclosure crisis as caused by the 1% manipulating the government to meet their needs at the expense of the needs of the 99%, then they are likely to want to change the policies that enable that vast accumulation of wealth.

Work to change systems of meaning takes support away from operations of power. An important part of an accountability democracy is shifting meanings such that people see an operation of power as unacceptable.

Responsibility

Accountability mechanisms also need to assign responsibility. If the problem exists in a cloudy world where everyone is responsible for everything, then no one can be held accountable for it. With both climate change and sweatshop labor, this issue of responsibility is one of the key sources of the trouble we have dealing with the problem.

If we want to have systems of accountability that are up to challenging the invisible powers we face, we need to find ways to park a problem at someone's doorstep. Reweaving the social fabric to tame the damaging powers we face requires that we stop the processes that generate those problems. And that requires that we find those who are most able to stop the problems, and requires that we hold them responsible to do so.

We are all responsible for the fabric of the society we inhabit, not necessarily in a legal sense, but in a moral sense. Following Young, we can say that we are morally responsible for the things we are connected to, to the extent that we have the power to influence them. And those with more power have more responsibility.

As we dig into the question of responsibility, it is important to remember that responsibility does not necessarily mean liable to legal sanction, it doesn't mean at fault, or blamable for a problem. Rather it means able to make a difference. Following Young, our responsibly is related out our "power, privilege, interest, and collective ability to make a difference."[1]

Developing an accountability mechanism requires that responsibilities get parked at a number of doorsteps. As we reweave the social fabric, there isn't one set of actions that offers a magic bullet to make a serious social problems go away. Instead, deep systemic change requires many actions at many levels. And that means setting up many accountability mechanisms, with many different claims of responsibility. Who is held responsible and what kind of accountability mechanism will be the most effective for solving any given problem is a strategic question.

In the case of police violence what is needed for a strong accountability mechanism seems to be fairly clear, at first glance. The person who pulled the trigger should be held liable for their action. If, upon investigation, it can be shown that the shooting was not justified, then that police officer should be held criminally liable for their action.

And yet, as activists work to change systems that allow for police murder, we start to see that there are multiple layers of responsibility. Firing and jailing one officer won't make huge difference if a department has a culture of racism and impunity embedded in it. Those fighting to change the system have wanted to also hold police chiefs responsible, so that actions are more likely to lead to systemic changes within a department. In the United States they have called for action on the part of the Federal Department of Justice, because sometimes local reformers do not have the power to force systemic change.

In a very connected world, there are many actors responsible for any given harm, and they are many different ways that those harms can be stopped. What is the best way to stop a given harmful process, and therefore where to park responsibility, has to do with dynamics of power.

Power

An accountability mechanism is only as good as the ability to enforce it. If a local police accountability commission finds a department in need of systemic change, that won't matter much if they are not able to make those changes happen. Many places have minimum wage laws and sanctions on the books against those who underpay workers. But those laws don't mean much if the authorities don't enforce them. The entities residing at that address that responsibility gets parked at need to have the power to stop the problem. And those monitoring their actions need to have the power to make them act responsibly to change the situation.

In order to create accountability mechanisms in the areas of concentrated and unaccountable power we have been looking at, there needs to be work on systems of meaning to give a claim moral authority, and to give a sense of who is responsible. But there also needs to be political action to transform institutionalized power relations, such that whatever is making a problem happen can be transformed to prevent it from happening in the future.

That work is often highly controversial and usually lies outside the framework of what is possible for people working in the world of NGOs funded by powerful entities.² Work done to develop accountability mechanisms needs to be deeply sensitive to the real operations of power in which it takes place. It needs to not shy away from hard questions of what it will take to hold power to account. And we need to be strategic about when to spend our political capital and when to play it safe and not challenge power.

If we add values, responsibility, and power to discussions of accountability, we will be much more able to understand the nature of the accountability mechanisms that already exist, and those which need to be developed to challenge the large-scale, elusive, contested, and slippery configurations of power we have been discussing. Challenging these configurations of power also requires that we do a bit to rethink the two standard parts of an accountability mechanism: voice and sanction.

Voice

Those calling for accountability mechanisms need to be mindful of the networks of power in which they operate. Is a call for justice based on a real grievance? Is it based on someone being on the underside of an illegitimate concentration of power? Is it based on real pain? In a world of unequal power, calls for accountability are often manipulative attempts by the powerful to expand or maintain their power. The voice side of an accountability mechanism needs to be investigated to see if it is an expression of a real pain, voiced with the intention of developing a real solution.

In the 1990s, President Bill Clinton pushed a set of draconian changes to the US welfare system under the title "The Personal Responsibility and Work Opportunity Act." Pandering to the sense that many white voters had that their tax moneys were going to support undeserving people of color, Clinton used the rhetoric of accountability to push millions of people off of welfare, and many of them into more serious poverty. At that time there was little evidence of people misusing the system, or of welfare causing them to lose a sense of personal responsibility.

In the United States right now, our system of voting rights is under an organized and concerted attack by the right under the guise of catching fraud. States are passing onerous voter identification laws, which make it much harder for low-income people to vote. The motive behind those actions is a very cynical attempt to suppress voting among populations that are likely to vote for Democrats.

Those same forces that have pushed for accountability in voting and welfare systems have also pushed for accountability in education. They were the forces behind the failed "No Child Left Behind" approach to education in the United States that forced school systems to spend huge amounts of money on testing, forced children to sit through stressful tests, took time away from learning, and which did not improve the quality of education.[3] In many countries with corrupt political systems anti-corruption campaigns can often become an opportunity to attack people working within government who have in some way challenged those with more power than themselves. These are all examples of pseudo-accountability.

Pseudo-accountability works by inciting a sense of grievance among the population, and by using the power that comes from the mobilization of resources, in terms of either electoral support or support for the actions of states or organizations to then accumulate more power. Pseudo-accountability makes the crisis of accountability worse. An important part of ending mass incarceration is to hold responsible those who incite panic for cynical reasons. In this case, what is needed is less an accountability mechanism and more the exposure of a mechanism of pseudo-accountability.

In all of these cases, calls for accountability were not initiated in response to the voicing of real worries. The rhetoric of accountability was used to disempower poor people and people of color, and those using that rhetoric new full well that they were not responding to real problems.

Authentic calls for accountability are set up to stop a real harm that people are voicing. To know if an accountability mechanism is authentic it is important to inquire if it is responding to a real voiced pain, and is responding in ways that are genuinely intended to alleviate that pain. Otherwise it is likely to be a case of pseudo-accountability.

Sanction

For an accountability mechanism to work, there needs to be someone with the power to make those responsible for a problem interrupt whatever harmful act they are able to stop. Often that power is not the power to punish or sanction but the power to influence. *Crucial Accountability* is a how-to book for managers trying to get accountability within the systems they control at a company. In it, the authors see the power in accountability as "social influence."[4] They argue that managers who punish are much less effective than ones who are able to get people to do their job by helping them to see how it is in their interest to do better.

The kinds of sanctions that exist in effective accountability mechanisms are only rarely about punishment. In the context of workplace management, a sanction might be writing an evaluation of an employee that asks them to do something differently. Just as the responsibility we are talking about here is not necessarily legal liability, so a sanction is not necessarily a punishment. Instead it is a consequence for an action that has the effect of changing a behavior.

Typically, we think of sanctions in terms of legal liability, as in fines and jail time. But a sanction can also be a loss of status, as when someone is not promoted at work or receives a negative performance evaluation; it can involve making public something that one wanted to remain private; it can involve changing the rules of the game; it can involve people pulling away from someone because you don't like what they have done.

Kinds of Sanctions for Effective Accountability Mechanisms

In the case of climate change, in order to bring global emissions down, all around the world, a variety of kinds of sanctions are being brought to bear on a variety of actors. Regulations, such as energy efficiency standards for buildings, are being passed by national governments; laws are being used to sanction those who violate those standards; market mechanisms, such as Canada's carbon tax, are being used to shift consumer and producer choices away from high-carbon products and production methods; protest movements, such as the one that challenged the Keystone XL and Dakota Access pipelines, raise the political cost of climate destroying actions; investigative journalists are getting the public to scrutinize the actions of the major fossil fuel corporations; elections are being won by people who are committed to changing laws; and people are demanding rights, such as a right to a healthy future.

Accountability mechanisms rely on at least these five types of sanction to work: law, regulation, markets, scrutiny, disruption, elections, and rights claims.[5] Each of these kinds of sanction is more easily used by those with more power than by those who are on the outside wanting to challenge concentrations of power. And yet for each of them, there are ways for anyone to use them to build accountability mechanisms that disrupt dominating systems of power and build accountability democracy.

Law

When looking to hold someone accountable, the first thought most people have is that they should be sanctioned by law. Legal mechanisms can easily be used by those with power to punish those who violate the laws of a given society. Legal mechanisms are harder to use for those with less power, or in circumstances where the powers being challenged are not those typically within a government's purview. But there are ways that law can be used by the less powerful to hold even transnational and slippery powers to account.

Public interest law firms often take on class action cases and use the legal system to sue corporate violators or governments. In 2016, a judge in Oregon allowed the Juliana versus US case to go forward, in which a group of children are suing the US government. They claim that by granting permission to oil companies to drill on public land, and other such decisions, the US government is taking away their right to a future. They are suing on the basis of the Ninth Amendment to the constitution which says that rights not mentioned in the constitution should be protected.

In *American Nuremberg* Rebecca Gordon asks what can be done to hold the United States accountable for war crimes committed during the administration of George W. Bush. She argues that best would be if international law functioned such that the United States could be brought to the International Criminal Court. That court grew out of the Nuremberg Trials at the end of the Second World War, and was intended to hold war criminals accountable.[6] But the United States never ratified the treaty that formed the International Criminal

Court, and in fact passed legislation making it illegal for the court to indict US citizens.

Some nations have begun to integrate issues of international concern into their legal purview. In 1998, Spanish Judge Baltazar Garzón indicted Augusto Pinochet for committing war crimes during his reign as dictator of Chile. The basis of the indictment was crimes against humanity. Those crimes are not limited by geographical jurisdiction.

Some of the major players in the administration of George W. Bush have not travelled internationally since ending their reign. Cheney, Rumsfeld, and Bush are all aware of the fact that there are judges in many countries who would love to hold them to account for their actions in the wars in Iraq and Afghanistan.

Gordon argues that the most likely way to hold those actors to account is a people's tribunal. During the Vietnam War, Bertrand Russell, Jean-Paul Sartre and several other prominent world citizens held a tribunal to indict the United States for crimes against humanity, committed during the Vietnam War.

If the people putting on such a tribunal are prominent enough, such a tribunal can change world opinion and make it very clear to history that the actions in question are deeply wrong. By setting the historical record straight, such tribunals can function as a disincentive to future war crimes. In this case, the rhetoric of law plays a powerful sanctioning role, even where an established legal system cannot be mobilized to play that part.

International law is developing in ways that begin to stretch beyond some of its old boundaries, and to take seriously the kinds of violation that have typically fallen between the cracks in our legal systems, and which often characterize the damaging powers we have been investigating.

Legal actions at a variety of levels, from the national in the case of *Juliana vs United States*, to the transnational, in the case of the trial against Pinochet, to the symbolic in the case of a people's tribunal, all attempt to constrain power by using the notion of legal norms, as well as actual legal processes, as mechanisms of sanction.

Regulation

In 2006, when California was debating AB 32—its landmark climate regulation—there were many people advocating for a system of cap and trade, where a market in greenhouse gas emissions would be created to make it profitable for corporations to reduce emissions. Arnold Schwarzenegger, who was the governor at the time, fought hard for most of the reductions to come from that cap and trade system. He was beat out by more progressive forces that were concerned about the ways that markets can be gamed. Instead, 80 percent of the emissions reductions called for by the law come from regulations, and only 20 percent come from the market-based cap and trade system.[7]

With a regulation, people who hold the levers of governmental power can decide on the best solution to a problem, can pass a law, such as emissions levels for cars, and can enforce that law through very tough sanctions, such as jail time and fines.

Many movements are focused on pressuring governments to pass regulations that are in the public interest, such as better police practices, food safety, emissions reductions, minimum wages, restrictions on finance capital, and so on. One does not need to control the state to be able to impact its regulations. What is needed is the ability to pressure those who do hold those levers to operate them in the interest of constraining power. Because the environmental movement was so strong when he was in office, some of the most important environmental legislation in the United States was passed during the presidency of Richard Nixon, who himself was very hostile to environmentalism.

Market

The recent period has been dominated by neoliberal ideology that encourages us to think of markets as the main way to get things done. For many years, and in many places, it has been hard to elect politicians who would act in the interest of low-wage workers, to get governments to pass strong labor laws, to have unions free to organize without harassment, or to have a healthy legal framework in which to operate. And so many campaigners have focused on market-based strategies for accountability rather than trying to get government regulations passed to solve problems.

Market-based social justice campaigns usually start with the voicing of a problem, such as, for example, the use of slave and child labor in the production of chocolate. An organization hears that voice, gives it meaning by, in this case, contrasting fair-trade chocolate with chocolate being made by slave and child labor. It holds consumers responsible for sanctioning the companies that use inhumane practices. And those companies are sanctioned by a market that prefers the chocolate being made by the more humane practices.

Important strategic questions to ask of such a fair-trade mechanism are the following: Does it set up a niche market to allow for good feelings among those who can afford to buy expensive products, while leaving the majority of producers unaffected? Does it change the lives of chocolate producers in significant ways? In this example, to know if there is an effective accountability mechanism, we need to ask if it results in there being less chocolate produced in inhumane ways. Sometimes social justice campaigners can promote accountability democracy through influencing markets, and sometimes those changes are only cosmetic.

Sometimes these market-based strategies work in concert with attempts to pass stronger regulations that companies have to work under, and efforts to get governments to enforce existing laws, and to elect people who will work toward those things. There are other times when the labor organizers who typically focus on those more state-based forms of accountability are frustrated by the efforts of human rights NGO's which can focus on destroying the reputation of a company, but which don't always yield on the ground results for workers. Often civil society-based strategies, such as mobilization of support and publicity and pressure campaigns within a low-wage country operate as a bridge between market, regulation, and legal strategies. [8]

Scrutiny

One of the most powerful parts of a campaign to get a government to pass regulations, to get someone held legally accountable, or to impact a market, is by putting them under a public spotlight. Any entity that relies on a good reputation, or a sense that its power is legitimate, can be vulnerable to being scrutinized.

Organizers, especially of social media campaigns, have sometimes made the mistake of supposing that scrutiny is always helpful for bringing a problem to account. Public scrutiny doesn't work against entities that don't care what you think about them. One example of a misguided attempt at scrutiny was the "Bring Back our Girls" campaign which was started when the Nigerian group Boko Haram, kidnapped over 200 girls. Boko Haram doesn't care if people in the West don't like it. In fact, a reputation as significant opponents of the West feeds its power. A public scrutiny campaign is only a mechanism for accountability for agents whose success depends on a good reputation.

In their article "Democracy in the Digital Communication Environment: A Typology," Ramón Feenstra and Andreu Casero-

Ripollés explore the types of scrutiny that are developing in the digital realm which can be used as monitory mechanisms for accountability. And they divide this work into four major types: "watchdog function, extraction and filtration of secret information, expansion of issues through alternative journalism, and extension of representation beyond parliaments."[9]

Trained journalists have been the main watchdogs in the modern period. That watchdog function is spreading to wider groups of people, as can be seen by the tremendous impact citizen videos have had on incidents of police murders. As digital technology spreads, so does the ability of all of us to work as watchdogs.

The work of Chelsea Manning, Edward Snowden, and the people behind the Panama Papers are examples of the monitoring function of making information available. The person who leaked the Panama Papers got access to millions of files from the law firm Mossack Fonseca and turned them over to journalists. It was up to the journalists to make sense of that information.

Feenstra and Casero-Ripollés argue that the internet is allowing much more unruly forms of journalism to proliferate and increasingly, the mainstream media is in the position of responding to issues that get surfaced by outsiders.

Finally, they argue that when people work to influence a political dynamic without being elected members of government, they are extending political power by demanding that systems be responsive to a set of unaddressed needs.

> New social movements, such as Occupy Wall Street, #Yosoy32, and Movimiento 15-M have played key roles in the extension of representation beyond parliaments. These citizen groups are mainly characterized by the use of digital technologies to challenge or alter the dominant, expected, accepted ways of conduct in society and politics.[10]

Power can be challenged through political action that puts pressure on unaccountable actors by shining a light on unjust actions. Their fourth form of scrutiny overlaps with the fifth approach to sanction on my list: disruption.

Disruption

Protest disrupts business as usual by drawing attention to a social issue. It causes those with dominating power to have to reconsider the calculus behind their actions. If police killings go largely unnoticed by the public, then an officer who is about to pull a trigger is not likely to worry about going to jail or losing her job. *Black Lives Matter* transformed what was considered routine and normal behavior into a socially significant moral wrong. Police chiefs and mayors have been held responsible, and the protests have strengthened the spines of those in positions of power to act to transform the cultures within police departments. All of these pieces, working together, can change the calculation of those about to perpetrate these violent crimes.

In San Francisco in 2016 there was a movement to get the mayor to fire the chief of police. The city had a police accountability system, but that system rarely worked. After a hunger strike, much protesting, and one more unjustified police murder, the mayor fired the chief of police, aiming to send a strong message to the department that practices need to change. That whole chain of events was set off by the vigilance of those who used protest actions to keep the public's attention on police murders.

While market-based mechanisms hold those with power to account by diminishing their ability to make a profit through sales, unions use strikes and other job actions to sanction companies by disrupting their ability to make a profit at the point of production. These actions sanction an employer directly, and where it hurts. In its famous Justice for Janitors campaign in the 1990s, the Service Employees International Union (SEIU) used a complex strategy that mobilized a variety of kinds of sanction and that dealt creatively with the problem of subcontracting. Many major corporations have their janitorial services done by small independent companies. The subcontracting is a way to avoid accountability for the people who provide their janitorial services.

SEIU ran highly theatrical disruption campaigns which were not aimed at shutting down production for the company. And they didn't target the subcontractors who were the direct employers of the janitors. Rather, they focused the campaigns on shaming the major employers that hired the subcontractors. Those major companies were vulnerable to the loss of prestige that scrutiny brings in a way not true for the subcontractors. They used disruption, but that disruption was not aimed at disrupting production as much as it was aimed at bringing scrutiny to a company's reputation, and thereby impacting its market share.

More traditional union campaigns disrupt production and cost a company money for all of the time that production is shut down. Strikes can be very effective and they bypass the state, holding a company directly to account for the ways it treats its workers.

In the classic 1978 book *Poor People's Movements: Why They Succeed and How They Fail*, Richard Cloward and Francis Fox Piven argue that action by poor people for social change is most effective when it is disruptive. The media tend to report on riots as senseless acts of frustration that do nothing more than destroy the communities of those who riot. Cloward and Piven did an analysis of the impacts of a variety of strategies taken by poor people to advocate for social change. They found that power holders tend to respond to disruption with serious reforms.[11] They point out that serious threats of disruption are a form of power held by the most marginalized members of a society. The movement's power comes from the way it changes the calculus of power holders and makes giving concessions to the poor easier than maintaining the current unjust system.

Elections

Elections are a mechanism for holding elected officials accountable to those they represent. If a party is not able to provide the results people want, their dissatisfaction gets fed back into the system by lower levels of votes the next time around.

And yet, there are many ways that the power of elections is limited in their ability to hold power to account. One important reason is the influence of money on elections. When politicians feel that they need to keep their donors happy to get reelected, they are likely to see those donors as their main constituents. And voters often have to choose between candidates, none of whom represent their interests, because without a lot of money candidates don't get traction.

Politicians are also not accountable to the citizens they are supposed to represent if the things that matter to people are controlled by forces other than the elected officials. In 2015, the people of Greece were not able to vote for a party that represented their interest in not being manipulated by the world's financial institutions. Those decisions were being made elsewhere. In Europe there is much talk about ways to make the European Union itself a more democratic and responsive body.[12]

Finding ways to make it such that the decisions that impact people's lives are things over which they have some power is one of the most challenging questions of our time. Traditional notions of representative democracy focus on elections as the main way to sanction power. Because of the ways that the damaging powers we face are larger, more contested, more elusive, and slipperier than the powers representative democracies are imagined to control, elections will increasingly be seen as only one among many mechanisms for developing accountability democracy.

Rights

> Right. 5 A legal, equitable, or moral title or claim to the possession of property or authority, or enjoyment of privileges or immunities etc.

In the era of accountability democracy, assertions of rights are increasingly used as effective ways to challenge power. They help to mobilize resistance to regimes of power on the part of civil society. Keane sees the *United Nations Declaration of Human Rights* as a crucially important tool for the development of new approaches to politics. He paraphrases Lebanese diplomat Charles Malik, one of the drafters of the declaration, as arguing,

> If states reneged on their commitments to human rights ... human beings would have no alternative but to take things into their own hands, by nurturing and protecting human rights with the help of families, places of worship, circles of friendship and other intermediate institutions spanning the entire chasm between the individual and the State.[13]

For Malik, claims of rights can be effective mechanisms for challenging the legitimacy of operations of power. Advocacy groups are increasingly using claims of rights to give value and meaning to an expressed pain, as a part of a campaign to solve problems. Often those groups play the barking-dog role in accountability, exposing injustices and violations of rights and giving them meaning and publicity. Others play the biting-dog role of challenging the practices in legal systems.

Of course, claiming to have a right does not necessarily mean that this right will be respected. In *Rights Justice and the Bounds of Liberty*, Joel Feinberg claims that those who advocate for human rights are

> urging upon the world community the moral principle that *all* basic human needs ought to be recognized as claims (in the customary *prima facie* sense) worthy of sympathy and serious consideration right now, even though, in many cases, they cannot yet plausibly be treated as *valid* claims, that is, as grounds of any other people's duties . . . . I accept the moral principle that to have an unfulfilled need is to have a kind of claim against the world, even if against no one in particular.[14]

Feinberg is comfortable with rights that are clearly enshrined in law, such as the First Amendment to the US constitution. He sees other kinds of rights, such as human rights, as functioning as a form of rhetorical claim that does not necessarily imply a duty to be fulfilled.

> When manifesto writers speak of them as if actual rights, they are easily forgiven, for this is but a powerful way of expressing the conviction that they ought to be recognized by states here and now as potential rights and consequently as determinant of *present* aspirations and guides to *present* policies. That usage, I think, is a valid exercise in rhetorical license.[15]

For him, an actual right is one that is correlated with someone's duty, like the duty of a state to provide housing, if there is a law that gives that right. The history of rights discourse involves a dynamic relationship between people claiming a right and rights getting enshrined in the culture as legitimate, or being used in soft ways to influence political discourse, and sometimes eventually getting enshrined in legal systems and enforced.

The landmark *Roe versus Wade* Supreme Court decision that legalized abortion in the United States was based on a right to privacy, which at that time was not settled in law as a recognized right. The Ninth Amendment to the US constitution allows for rights not specifically listed in the constitution to be protected. *Roe v. Wade* used the Ninth Amendment to claim a right to privacy as a significant part of US law.

The US legal system generally only respects negative rights: rights to be left alone and not be interfered with. Positive rights, such as the right to water and health care, are enshrined in the *United National Declaration of Human Rights*. Those rights are seen as legally significant in some countries and not in others.

A right is a moral claim, but before it is enshrined in a functioning system of law it has a utopian element to it. It is only productive if it can eventually be parked at someone's doorstep as their responsibility to fulfill. A claim to a right is a step in the development of an accountability mechanism, where values and voice raise a problem as the responsibility of some agent to do something. That accountability mechanism is only complete when that responsibility is taken up as an action that sanctions those perpetuating the problem, and when there is power to make that sanction stick in a meaningful way that constrains power.

In *The Human Rights Enterprise*, William T. Armaline, Davita Silfen Glasberg, and Bandana Purkayastha claim that rights operate through a dynamic process. Citizens of the world, and social movements, play roles at least as important as governments in realizing our rights. They use the concept of the human rights enterprise to name that complex multipart dynamic that moves a right from being an empty piece of rhetoric to being an effective tool for social change.

The process through which human rights are defined and realized, including but not limited to the legal instruments and regimes often authorized by international elites. The human rights enterprise includes both legal, statist approaches to defining and achieving rights through agreements among duty-bearing states, and social movement approaches that manifest as social struggles over power, resources, and political voice. The human rights enterprise offers a way to conceptualize human rights as a terrain of social struggle, rather than a static, contingent legal construct.[16]

Rights are an important part of accountability. They are one of the most important mechanisms for turning pain into something that is seen as wrong and in need of action. Rights discourse is a powerful set of principles for translating suffering into a value-laden framework as a wrong that must be addressed.

Feedback Loops

For an accountability mechanism to function, there needs to be feedback between the actions that cause harm and agents with the ability to prevent that harm from happening in the future. The five elements of an accountability mechanism—voice, values, responsibility, power, and sanction—need to exist in a dynamic and productive relationship with one another.

In organizations where people work together, whether in a hierarchical workplace with a manager, or in a democratic organization, if a person does something wrong one of the most important things for others to do is to let that person know that the wrong action was noticed. An open system, where it seems that actions have no consequences, is devastating to the functioning of a system.[17]

With a feedback loop, a system is improved by the consequences of an action being brought into relationship to what caused the original action. In his article from *Wired* magazine, "Harnessing the Power of Feedback Loops,"[18] Thomas Goetz argues that society can be improved by the intentional use of feedback loops. He starts his article with the simple example of a traffic sign that shows drivers their speed. These signs are often used in the United States near school zones. They bring the driver's behavior of speeding to their consciousness in ways that make them see the consequences of their actions. Studies have found that this leads to real changes in behavior.

Goetz breaks a feedback loop down into four main elements: evidence, relevance, consequences, and action. In his example, the evidence is: "The radar-equipped sign flashes a car's current speed." Second is relevance: "The sign also displays the legal speed limit—most people don't want to be seen as bad drivers." The third element consequences: "People are reminded of the downside of speeding, including traffic tickets and the risk of accidents." Finally, the fourth comes action: "Drivers slow an average of 10 percent—usually for several miles. The individual has to engage with all of the above and act—thus closing the loop and allowing that new action to be measured."[19]

What is happening here is that the result of the driver's action, the fact of how fast they are going, is brought to their consciousness. A speedometer is also a feedback mechanism; it feeds back to our vision the results of how much we step on the accelerator. But most of us don't think consciously of our speed very often. In this particular example, by bringing the reality of the driver's speed to their consciousness, the driver pauses and thinks about the consequences of their action, and adjusts their action accordingly.

When I buy a piece of clothing it is very hard for me to see the connections between my action and the lives of the people who made that article of clothing. When I drive my car, I don't see the land that was destroyed to make the gas, or the fires that are caused when the emissions from my car destroy the atmosphere. When I vote for politicians who speak to my fears, I don't see that as leading to people going to jail and the ways that destroys communities.

Some of the lack of feedback in our contemporary society has to do with living on a large scale, where we don't live day to day with the people who are impacted by our actions. Some of it has to do with the complex nature of the technology we use. But it is also fostered by pro-capitalist ways of thinking.

Pro-capitalist Thought and Feedback Loops

Ways of thinking that support capitalism rests on the principles that we are each responsible for ourselves; that intentional, collective decision-making doesn't work; and that the more we let decisions be made by the market the better off everyone will be. This philosophy encourages us to not think in holistic and systemic ways. Each actor is supposed to pursue his self-interest and the invisible hand of the market is supposed to make all of those individual decisions lead to the best outcomes for everyone. Markets are a powerful feedback mechanism, and pro-capitalist thought encourages us to not rely on other forms of feedback.

Mainstream economic thought is based on the belief that markets generally work, that the price of a product will reflect its costs, and that desirable things will be brought forward by the market and less desirable ones will be disfavored. Economists have developed the concept of externalities to deal with the cases when this is not so.

If a textile plant pollutes the air and water, and its owners don't have to pay for the health impacts of that pollution, they have externalized the costs of that action. Mainstream economists like the idea that everything has a natural price, and they imagine that generally all of the costs of making something are reflected in its price. Markets provide the feedback needed to match people's desires with the things they want, based on the prices they are willing to pay. For them an externality is an exceptional case, and one role of government is to close the feedback loops when social problems are caused by externalities by making producers pay for them.

In the case of climate change, a carbon tax is a way of adding the cost to the environment of the burning of fossil fuels to the cost of our gas. This can be a very effective way to add the needs of society into the market for gasoline. It can incentivize alternative fuels by making them more cost competitive, and it can lead to energy conservation, as high prices often lead to cutting back on consumption. But passing a carbon tax is a very hard thing to do politically when people believe that, as consumers, they should be able to buy for the lowest price possible, and that the government should not mess with markets. And, it is actually a very inefficient way to get people to pollute less. Developing public transportation, incentivizing electric cars, and regulating emissions are much more efficient ways to reduce the pollution cause by gas cars.

Rather than being an exception, it is a routine and pervasive part of capitalist markets that prices do not reflect the social costs of a product. Producers are generally only asked to pay the prices for the inputs they use to make the things they make, the factories, the land a factory is on, the wages of the employees, and so on.

They are not asked to pay the cost of pollution, of the disruption caused by the changes they make in neighborhoods, for the housing needs of their employees, for the devastation caused by the low wages they pay, for the negative effects on the political system that come from their favoring politicians who work in their interests. The social cost of poverty in Bangladesh is not included in the price of my clothing as a cost. In fact, that poverty is reflected in the low price as something good.

Many of Walmart's workers are too poor to afford to eat well or have health care, and so they rely on government benefits. An economist could say that with its low wages Walmart has externalized the social cost of its labor. But generally, those social costs of Walmart's production are seen as not relevant to the picture of Walmart's economic behavior and not as part of its responsibility. The concept of externality is rarely mobilized to hold these actions to account.

When markets don't work to match desires with goods, and when products don't reflect their real costs to produce, economists call that market failure. One example of a market failure is low-income housing. Where I work, in the Silicon Valley, there is a tremendous economic boom going on. That has led to a shortage of moderate- and low-income housing. Low-income people are being displaced and forced to leave the area. Many of my students were involved in a campaign for rent stabilization to limit the rate of rent increases so that people would not be forced to leave. Opponents said that rent stabilization was irrational because it distorted the market. Their belief is that if property owners can charge a market rate then housing will be built.

The problem with this argument is that it is not very profitable to build housing for low-income people. There is "demand" for it, in the sense that people desperately want it. But markets do not respond to that sort of demand. They respond to "effective demand" which is desire backed by money.

Economists tend to see market failure and externalities as fairly rare. But critics of capitalism see them as chronic. It is a normal aspect of a capitalist market that those with the power to set wages will set them as low as they can. Those who want livable wages need to be part of a movement to fight for them. And if we want housing for low-income people, someone needs to be paid to build it. The market is not interested in people without money.

Mechanisms, such as taxes on the negative result of free markets, or regulating minimum wages, are ways to mitigate against the worst effects of a society where major decisions are made by markets. But that work has an uphill battle as pro-capitalist thinking encourages us to believe that, generally, markets work for the social good and that generally regulation and taxes are to be avoided.

Markets are one limited type of feedback loop. They work well to match the desires of people who have money with products that are pleasing to them. But markets can't serve society well on their own because of the pervasive nature of externalities, market failures, and the lack of demand of those without money. Taming the damaging powers embedded in a market-based economic system requires that the processes through which markets are created be exposed, and it requires other systems of control such as regulations and deeper social transformations.

Reform and Revolution

Whenever conversations arise about the problems inherent in capitalism, it is easy for the conversation to come to an end, since almost no one thinks we are on the verge of eliminating capitalism. This problem is worsened by a tendency among opponents of capitalism to think of it as something like an organic whole that must be overthrown all at once and which cannot be changed in significant ways short of revolution.

In my book *Getting Past Capitalism: History, Vision, Hope*, I argue that rather than seeing capitalism as a system that needs to be overthrown, it is more productive to understand it as a social formation, as a set of processes, constituted by a variety of forms of agency that need to be understood and challenged in a variety of ways. Getting past capitalism involves a variety of operations of accountability democracy.

There are many ways we can disrupt the reproduction and expansion of capitalist aspects of our society. We diminish capitalism through real practical challenges to the transnational ruling class, such that, for example, the institutions that are destroying the Greek economy should be required to work under a different set of rules. We also disrupt the move to a more capitalist society when we develop viable alternatives in the here and now, such as worker owned cooperatives, to show that other ways to organize production are possible. We can resist having our sense of self be constituted as capitalist-desiring subjects. And we can develop systems where our needs are taken care of, such as national health care, which reduce people's dependencies on a job in capitalist wage labor to get our needs met.[20]

People working for social justice often make a distinction between reform and revolution. Reforms, they claim, are changes that blunt the pain of a problem, but which don't solve it. One example of this is shelters for homeless people. As long as there is not enough decent housing for low-income people, people will be homeless, and will need shelters. Shelters are good because they ameliorate pain, but they don't solve the problem of homelessness. Really solving the problem involves finding ways for everyone to have access to decent permanent housing.

Many argue that a revolution that overthrows the existing power structures is the way to real, permanent, solutions to problems such as the ones we have been discussing. The debate between revolution and reform gets at an important set of issues: that some solutions get to the root causes of problems and can lead to that problem being solved in ways that others do not. But the idea of revolution often leads to political paralysis, as people only want to engage in actions that are aimed at "overthrowing the system." But you can't overthrow a market; you can't overthrow the transnational ruling class; you can't overthrow processes of dehumanization; and overthrowing a government does not automatically create a state that is accountable to its people.

Those ideas of overthrow within the anti-capitalist world have tended to be mixed up with ideas of overthrowing governments, as if they were the same thing. And yet, as anti-capitalists have come to power in many countries, either through revolutions, such as in Cuba in 1959, or elections, as in Venezuela in 2002, those countries have remained constrained by the capitalist world they are a part of.

More productive than the metaphor of overthrow, it is the metaphor of reweaving the social fabric. Rather than being stuck in a binary choice between reform and revolution, it is more helpful to focus on revolutionary reforms: changes that are part of a process of challenging unaccountable configurations of power and holding power to account.

Conclusion

Challenging power, and developing ways to hold it to account, requires a serious analysis of the sources of a problem and strategic thinking about the best ways to develop accountability mechanisms. There is no magic bullet to challenging power. Sometimes when a movement develops momentum it can be fast and can feel like what people mean when they call a change a revolution. But most of the time the work of challenging power feels incredibly slow and requires huge efforts for small gains. Whether one is lucky enough to be working in a time when change is coming quickly or has the strength of commitment to stay in the game when it is slow, the path to significant social change remains the same. We need to analyze what are the actions one can take that are likely to make a significant and lasting difference and work to set up functioning accountability mechanisms that shift the balance of power that undergirds unjust operations of power.

While most struggles to hold power to account are in themselves small, they can be significant if they add up to lasting change in the social fabric. Each of these actions can, if successful, be a part of transforming the social fabric such that power is less concentrated and less able to build on itself and accumulate. We can create accountability mechanisms such that people who are harmed by a system of power have the ability to voice their pain; the pain is understood as morally wrong; the wrong is seen as someone's responsibility to do something about; and that someone does something; and has the power to actually change the social pattern that caused the harm.

None of that can happen if the links in the chains of causality that make terrible things happen in this world are seen as separate entities. If every link in the chain between myself as a consumer and the person who made my clothes is seen as a discrete action, caused by a morally neutral market, then there is no hope for developing systems of accountability that prevent my clothes from being made in ways that cause buildings to fall on people and kill them. For that, we need to see how those links are connected, and the connections need to be more than linear, they need to have healthy systems of feedback between them.

Challenging the powers we face will involve developing effective and well-targeted accountability mechanisms. Those mechanisms must be developed with a good understanding of the powers they are up against and must be strategically designed to be effective. Using them will often push us outside of the comforts of the systems we inhabit, many of which were deigned to reproduce the very powers that need to be challenged.

Our moral philosophies and systems of governance need to be aligned with the real nature of the powers we are confronting. Kantian ethics asks us to be thoughtful participants in an orderly world. What we need now is an ethics for a tragically disordered world. To be an ethical person in the present context requires more than individual ethical consumption choices. Rather, it requires us to take responsibility for making a difference where we can. Questions of politics need to be understood broadly. Political work is work that transforms accumulations of power. Government is a part of that, but government is only one location where power is concentrated, and where power can be held to account.

The concept of accountability mechanisms can help us understand the actions that are taken to challenge all four types of damaging powers we have been investigating. Transnational institutions, such as the World Trade Organization (WTO), and transnational corporations, such as Exxon-Mobil, can be delegitimized by targeted protests; their actions can be shown to be unacceptable. Powers of government and law can be mobilized to limit their behavior. The aspects of an accountability mechanism that are the most difficult for challenging these large-scale operations of power are responsibility and power.

Because transnational institutions operate at a scale larger than national governments, those governments are often not powerful enough to challenge them. The protests in Seattle in 1999 to challenge the World Trade Organization (WTO) relied mostly on giving voice to the critique of the WTO. Most people had never heard of the WTO and had no idea of the undemocratic nature of the policies it propagated. Exposing this to the light of day then put pressure on the governments that supported it. Responsibility for the regulation of the WTO was parked at the door of politicians who supported it, and once support for the WTO became a very unpopular position, politicians were vulnerable to being sanctioned by voters.

In the case of the powers invested in government, accountability mechanisms can be used to win the contest of power over whose interests a government serves. The influence of money in elections can be exposed through voice. Power can be shifted by mobilizing resources other than money to elect people. Disruption can be used to pressure lawmakers to not enact undemocratic policies, and the sanction of electing other people can be used against politicians who don't serve the public interest. Challenging the power invested in government requires that we see government as a site of contest and not assume it to function in neutral ways. Those seeking accountability democracy need to enter that contest for power.

The unaccountable power hidden in markets can be exposed and markets can be regulated in ways that limit their power. What is challenging in developing accountability mechanisms to deal with slippery operations of power such as markets is that they are invisible, and it is hard to know where to park responsibility.

Work done to change how Economics 101 is taught, such that more people understand the mythical nature of the "free market," is important for authorizing the voice of those who want to reregulate markets in ways that serve human interests. To the extent that people understand that markets are always being regulated and reregulated, challenges to particular regulations of markets can more easily gain the power that comes from popular support.

And those who set the rules for markets can be exposed for shaping markets in ways that enable unjust accumulations of power. The fight for a fifteen dollar an hour minimum wage in the United States is one such struggle that attempts to regulate the labor market such that the floor for wages is high enough that people can live decent lives.

Slippery operations of power can be made accountable by showing the ways that they are the results of the real choices of real social actors, rather than being natural and unchanging.

Finally, work can be done to shift the meanings that inform our lives and construct our senses of self. This requires mostly work on the value aspects of an accountability mechanism. Exposing the operations of power hidden in our systems of meaning requires that we denaturalize the self and accept that our desires are social constructs. Challenging this configuration of power requires looking to the sources of who is trying to shape our desires for their own interests. It also requires work voicing alternative ways of understanding the world and creating forms of meaning and desire that make the world sensible from a perspective of a fair distribution of power. An important step in challenging elusive operations of power, embedded in systems of meaning, is to understand them as operations of power, and to engage in battles that have no clear target, and which are themselves often elusive in nature.

Since the old systems to hold and constrain power, such as the nation-state, are decreasingly the places where power is enacted, our efforts to constrain power need to be rethought if we want to develop accountability democracy. We need to develop real and effective strategies that can be used to challenge the damaging powers we face and create systems that will breakup, hold, and constrain them.

7
Building Accountability Democracy

It seems to me that compassion and empathy are important here. We need to make room for everyone in this world to have what they need. When I see pictures of people drowning in the Mediterranean, and I hear what the politicians in Europe say about them, I am afraid. That could be me they're talking about. How are those people supposed to live if it gets too hot for them to grow anything?

I think so much about global warming. And it makes me feel powerless. I am starting to do what I can. I've changed all my light bulbs, and I am eating less red meat. I was happy to hear that in Paris they were able to agree on taking some action. But it does seem that some people there were probably asking for too much, and that never helps with making an agreement. We need to all bend a little bit and meet each other halfway.

Anything less than a serious commitment to keep warming below 1 degree Celsius is essentially a death warrant for millions of us who call the African continent home. Hundreds of thousands of people have already died or have been and forced to migrate as a result of the changing conditions. The problem

can be completely solved without anyone in the Global North losing the comforts and pleasures to which you have grown accustomed. It merely takes a shifting of your technologies. Of that you are surely capable. Unfortunately for all of us, your political systems are not so forward looking or clever. They are machines developed for slavery, colonialism, dehumanization, and exploitation. They were exquisitely designed to profit from us, and that is what they will, most likely, continue to do. And your people will feel aggrieved when we try to leave those areas which you have made uninhabitable.

You are going to kill the goose that is laying our golden eggs. This whole thing is just an excuse cooked up by people who want socialism to get in there and muck up the economy with job killing regulations.

My part of the world is going up in flames. And you are sitting on your ass having your deluxe little life and just letting it happen. You are too cowardly to help with the things that need to be done.

Perhaps you could invite the CEO of Shell Oil to spend some time sitting in an Ogoni forest, so he could see the humanity and the suffering of the people who live there. He might have his heart opened, and he might wish to stop the devastation. As a member of the human species, he is in fact likely to be moved by the reality he sees. And yet, sadly, his job is to return the greatest profits for his shareholders. If he were to suddenly believe in a world of peace and love he would have to lose his position. If his bosses didn't fire him, they could be held liable for not fulfilling the corporation's mission.[1]

...

In the beginning God created the universe. It was spectacular in every way. There were beautiful trees, plants, multicolored birds, and animals filled the lands with their cries and songs of delight. In the sea, the colorful fishes and marine life illuminates the vast ocean bodies. The world was indeed impeccable. Then he decides that all of these creatures needed a leader. Alas, the creation of mankind, the dawn of a new era . . . . The threat from climate change is real, urgent, serious and is growing overnight.

Let me tell you my story to bring it close to home. I hail from the beautiful province of Tailevu, in a small village in Wainibuka called Naivicula, which is in Viti Levu, the largest island in Fiji. Early in 2016 we were hit by one of the strongest cyclones to ever strike Fiji, the strongest in the southern hemisphere. My home, my school, our source of food, water, money, was totally destroyed. My life was in chaos. I asked myself, why is it happening? Why is the cyclone getting stronger? What am I going to do? . . . My once beautiful village, I once called home, is now a barren and empty wasteland. Months that follows, summer temperatures continue rising, reduction of soil moisture, turning our land infertile. Trees not bearing fruits in its usual season, water bodies getting dry each day. Fishes, shrimps, prawns, eels, dead on lakes and river. I feel the pain, the remorse, the anger, the loss, the terror, the insecurity, worthless and useless, as I watched everything around me turning from green to yellow then brown. A sure sign that we are dying. Facts indicate that a total of 40,000 homes were damaged or destroyed by this monstrous disaster.

There is an eye opener for us as individuals, communities, nations, and also as a global village . . . . The blaming and waiting days are over. We need to act now. . . . Speeches and talks will not solve the problem. . . . This is sure not going to happen if we pretend and wait for others. It is time to unite to move forward together. We have heard, we have seen, we have witnessed, we were victims. Now it is time to conquer. Ladies and gentleman, systems may change, human can change, but climate change is here to stay unless you do something about it. With these words let us be more environmental oriented and help restore our spectacular mother earth.[2]

There are an infinite number of paths we can each take to strengthen accountability democracy. Building accountability democracy means working to develop mechanisms to challenge unaccountable power. Developing those mechanisms involves organizing and that organizing, when it is successful, often develops into social movements. This chapter takes the examples of major social problems we have been investigating, such as sweatshops, police violence, climate change, and the Greek economic crisis, and looks at real work that is happening in the present to solve that problem. It no longer looks at each problem as an example of one configuration of power. Here, each example is looked at in terms of the actual work being done to challenge the variety of configurations of power at play.

Each example also is elaborated in ways that help us to see how all five aspects of an accountability mechanism are part of the work of challenging the powers that constitute the problem being addressed, and the ways that movements working on that problem mobilize effective forms of feedback. Each example is also taken as an opportunity to dig a bit more deeply into Iris Marion Young's argument that responsibility is related to our "power, privilege, interest, and collective ability to make a difference."[3] In these examples we can see that actors located at different parts of these struggles each have different responsibilities and capacities, and can play different, and complementary, roles.

Preventing Future Building Collapses

In response to the Rana Plaza disaster, a coalition of labor and monitoring groups came together and by May 2013 were able to get most of the main retailers and unions working in Bangladesh to agree to binding commitments for building safety standards, the *Accord for Fire and Building Safety in Bangladesh*. While it has clearly not stopped the problem of unsafe labor conditions, it was a significant step forward in a broad strategy for ending sweatshop conditions.

Often, anti-sweatshop action takes place either on the production side, with labor unions calling for strikes and other actions to punish a producer, or on the consumer side, where groups have tended to target brand names. In this case the two sides worked together. Consumption-based organizing often casts a wide net that is hard for companies to escape, but if a company's image is tarnished it may end up producing less, and thus employing fewer people. Unions which focus on the production side usually know how hard they can fight without companies leaving because they can't make a profit. But over time, union activity can lead to companies leaving and finding a different place to set up shop where the labor conditions are more favorable. The challenge for organizers has been how to keep globalized production from flowing to where conditions are the lowest, and yet also to keep production happening.

In this case, a coalition of agents from both sides led to significant changes.

> The Clean Clothes Campaign educated consumers about the brands sourcing from Rana Plaza and mobilized them to put pressure on brands to sign the Accord. But the Accord also reflects the mobilization of production power, as global unions pushed for going beyond surface-level changes towards a more substantive

agreement. The result is an unprecedented legally binding agreement between the global union federations, IndustriALL and UNI Global Union, Bangladeshi trade unions and over 190 ready-made garment retailers and brands.[4]

As part of the agreement, brands agreed to maintain the volumes they had been purchasing for the next for five years, thus giving an incentive to invest in safety and decent buildings.

In terms of Young's "power, privilege, interest, and collective ability to make a difference," the workers at the Bangladeshi factories had the greatest interest in improved conditions and had a privileged insight into understanding what needed to be changed. But they were the least privileged actors in this drama, as they were the ones most likely to lose their employment if things went badly, or to suffer from dangerous working conditions if the Accord did not get implemented. They had some power to make a difference through their threat of withdrawing their labor.

The consumers had the most privilege, in that they had almost nothing to lose in this situation, and yet they also had the least at stake, so their interest level was low, and their power was quite diffuse. Their power would not amount to much at all if it were not mobilized by organizations that could use consumer boycott as a threat.

The consumer-based organizations had quite a bit of power, through their threat of consumer action, to get a place at the table to negotiate an agreement. Their collective ability to make a difference is related to the sophistication of the strategic path they chose.

The union-based organizations had a strong interest in success. But because of the flexibility of globalized production to move when conditions don't suit them, their power to get improved conditions through striking is limited. And yet when that threat is developed in conjunction with consumer-based organizations, their power is quite significant.

We can see the whole set of actions related to Rana Plaza, from the initial collapse, to the signing of the Accord, as an effective exercise in accountability democracy. The strategy taken with the Accord took seriously the formation of power that faced the Bangladeshi workers. The workers were up against global labor markets that have developed in ways that allow capital to flow where it will gain the greatest profits. Globalized production is a strategy for avoiding the power of labor. The Bangladeshi government has been operating almost entirely on the side of the factory and land owners. Consumers may care about labor conditions, and feel badly about what happened, but unless that care is mobilized into an effective collective strategy, individual action does not change the behavior of the producers.

The organizers used the attention that was focused on the disaster to get some significant concessions from the industry, and while the Accord may not last, it was a helpful step for long-term organizing to end sweatshop labor. As an exercise in accountability democracy, this fight was successful in all five of the elements necessary for an accountability mechanism:

Values: when the collapse happened people all over the world were horrified and were inclined to see the problem as caused by unfair conditions for labor, and not just as an accident.

Voice: the problem was discussed and analyzed in the news media all around the world, and was amplified by anti-sweatshop organizations.

Responsibility: organizers in the consumption based, as well as the production based, organizations decided to focus on the retailers as the ones responsible for ensuring that the conditions at the factories were up to a certain level. The Bangladeshi state was not focused on as the main agent to ensure the standards, because they are not vulnerable to the pressures that the two types of organizations are able to bring to bear on brand name retailers.

Sanction: The companies are vulnerable to coordinated national-scale strikes as well as consumer boycotts to support those strikes if companies violate the Accord.

Power: As long as they keep consumers and workers engaged, the organizations have the power to sanction the retailers for noncompliance.

There is a myriad of possible ways to prevent future building collapses, such as the one that killed Rina Rehman at Rana Plaza. Deciding which path to take requires a careful analysis of the complex configurations of power one is confronting, the roles and capacities of the players in the struggle, as well as a careful analysis of how each of the five elements of an accountability mechanism can be brought to bear on the situation. Because of the global attention to the disaster, those working for the Accord were able to get significant improvements in working conditions in Bangladesh. While it clearly doesn't eliminate capitalism, the Accord does shape the market in ways that are less damaging than before. It challenges the race to the bottom by setting a floor.

In this case, one aspect of the formation of power that needed to be challenged was the unaccountable and slippery nature of markets. By impacting the ability of the market to determine working conditions, the power of the market has been challenged. Accountability democracy is developed through challenging networks of power and transforming them such that oppressive configurations of power are undermined.

The power that comes from markets operating as if no one were responsible for them is challenged when markets are reshaped to be less damaging to human needs. And if the strategy used in the Accord is able to be replicated by others, using a combination of producer and consumer-based strategy, then its significance is even greater.

Preventing Police Violence

Since the launching of the hashtag #BlackLivesMatter, there has been increasing attention to the centuries-old problem of police violence against Black people. In 2015, the Movement for Black Lives came together as a coalition of over fifty organizations dedicated to challenging the oppression of Black people in the United States. That organization is doing important work helping orient and support local actions. Because police are generally controlled by local municipalities, with little federal or state oversight, much of the crucial work to transform police practices remains local. There has been worry that those actions would continue to run up against prosecutors unwilling to challenge police and juries indifferent to the value of Black Lives. The worry has been that they would remain on the voice side of an accountability mechanism, and not be able to move to having sanctions that would really shift the balance of power, and thus change future outcomes.

In 2013, in response to a wide range of abuses community members are subjected to by the New York Police Department (NYPD), a coalition of over 200 community based organizations, Communities United for Police Reform, worked to pass a set of Community Safety Act bills that ban discriminatory profiling.[5] The coalition is continuing to work in New York City to develop the sanctions side of accountability for the NYPD. They have continued to work for several pieces of legislation, as they also continue to expose oppressive police practices.

After Eric Garner's death, the NYPD engaged in some retraining, and reasserted its already existing ban on the chokehold that was used to kill Garner. At that time, the chief of police was William Bratton, who was the inventor of the broken windows approach to policing, which targets communities of color with constant harassment for small infractions, such as jay walking, or selling individual cigarettes. In 2016, Bratton resigned, as a result of pressures being brought to bear by the movement for police reform. In 2019, officer Daniel Pantaleo was finally fired from the NYPD.

The root cause of the problem that the movement is dealing with is that Black people are not recognized in their full humanity in US society. As the movement challenges individual acts of police violence, it also needs to keep doing the work of transforming the meaning of humanity that underlies the problem. The mere act of holding police officers accountable is a step in that transformation. By treating each death as an assault on the humanity of Black people, each protest is an assertion of that humanity, and a challenge to that underlying system of meaning.

The families of people murdered by police are powerful agents in reminding everyone of the pain caused by those deaths, as they call for empathy and humane treatment. And yet those family members generally aren't taken seriously by the power structures that might hold police to account and change the way communities of color are policed. The system is allowed to continue to act as if those lives don't matter.

People in the broader Movement for Black Lives, and local organizations such as the 200 groups in New York's Communities United for Police Reform are a bit more distanced from the pain than are family members, and have more privilege to take up strategies for organizing to transform the system that allows these murders. The movement is in a position to formulate goals for collective actions. They analyze the formation of power they are confronting and decide what kind of action, directed where, is most likely to change the power dynamics which allow for police murder.

People in the general population can chose to join the movement, and engage in collective action, and can support politicians, such as the members of the New York City Council who are working to pass these bills that hold the NYPD to account. And the public can shift its assessment of the humanity in Black people, such that significant outrage is mobilized to get the system to react and have the legal structures function to protect Black lives.

Prosecutors, mayors, and chiefs of police are important power holders, who could change the rules of the game to stop the problem from happening. They have the power to fire officers who show a disregard for Black lives. They can institute policies that stop the police from functioning in low-income communities of color as an occupying force. They can use all of their prosecutorial power to throw the book at officers who kill innocent people.

As an exercise in accountability democracy, the Movement for Black Lives has been very successful at the voice side of an accountability mechanism. They have drawn attention to instances of police murder as morally wrong, and not just as something that happens in the heat of hard police work; they have made that message as loud as possible through protest action; they have begun to park the responsibility at the doorstep of local politicians in each city where a murder has taken place, and they have demanded changes from the politicians who hold governmental power in those places.

In many localities they are beginning to gain traction on the sanctions side of accountability: they are working with legislators to pass laws, to fire police chiefs, and to develop accountability mechanisms within police departments. They are also having some success at changing the role that people think the police should have in their relations with communities of color. The power embedded in systems of meaning that devalue some lives are challenged when movements successfully insist that people with power act as if those lives do matter.

Accountability for the Climate Crisis

The crisis in the health of our climate is being addressed by millions of people all around the world. New technologies are being developed, new regulations are being put into place, effective systems of public transportation are growing, and renewable energy is quickly replacing fossil fuel-based energy. And yet at the same time, in the United States, the Koch brothers funded network of think tanks and fake grassroots organizations and has captured large percentages of state and federal politicians.[6] Those politicians routinely deny the reality of climate change, and face primary challenges if they don't toe that line.

Scientists worked for years to show that climate change was a problem. It then took more work to have it seen that the problem was not just a neutral outcome of normal social processes, but rather, as something morally wrong that needed to be stopped. The next step in that process was to hold someone responsible. That work has taken many years, and is still being debated all around the world.

Part of the malaise people feel around the climate crisis is based on the fact that society has not completely settled on who to hold responsible for it. Many people end up blaming themselves, and just feeling badly whenever they think of the subject, or making changes to how they live their private lives. There is a logic to the claim that if my actions create greenhouse gas emissions, then I am responsible for the climate crisis, and that I can solve it through my individual actions.

For many people that logic has led to a personal accountability mechanism, where they see the problem and choose to fly less, eat less red meat, and consume fewer wasteful products such as bottled water. Some significant change does come from each of us holding ourselves responsible. And for many people this is the kind of accountability that makes the most intuitive sense.

If we look at individual lifestyle changes in light of this analysis of accountability mechanisms, we can see that the voice is there, the values are there, the responsibility is there, and there is a nice sanctions mechanism we can each set up for ourselves. We can set up personal incentives for meeting our carbon footprint goals. And the power is there as we are able to punish and reward ourselves to keep ourselves compliant.

Where this accountability mechanism goes wrong is on the aspect of responsibility. In this case, the one held responsible, the individual as consumer, is not really able to stop the problem. Those advocating for an individual lifestyle change as a path to significant social change have trouble showing that their individual actions will cause sufficient enough changes, quickly enough, that the problem will actually stop. Even if a given person's emissions went to zero, the climate crisis would continue.

There are many arguments among environmentalists on this question, and those in favor of the position that the path to social change is an aggregation of individual changes often argue that individual actions add up to more than their impact on the individual, because one person can be a role model for others. Lifestyle changes often do spread and one's actions sometimes do influence the actions of others. The weakness of this approach is that it is not enough to achieve the large-scale changes needed at a fast enough pace to avoid the worst catastrophic outcomes.

The presumption that my individual change will change the world is, at least in part, based on the logic of the invisible hand of the market. The logic of the market says that when I buy blue shoes, I am causing more blue shoes to be produced. In the ideal of the capitalist market, individual consumer choices are believed to naturally cause there to be more of what we like. If I don't buy a gas guzzler for a car, there will be fewer gas guzzlers produced. With our market behavior we vote with our feet through the choices we make. But very few aspects of our world operate like an idealized market.

In the United States, one could argue that cars must be better than buses because you can see how people are voting with their feet by choosing to drive individual cars. But people won't ride a system of public transportation until it is good enough meet our needs. Many cities, such as Bogotá Colombia, have systems of public transportation that are more attractive to use than private cars. And they didn't get that way as a result of people voting with their feet. Policymakers made decisions and took risks to invest in the system on the belief that once it was good enough, people would use it.

Many of the causes of greenhouse gas emissions exist in large systemic structures that can't be changed by individual market choices. The sources of power for our electric company, the availability of housing near transit, good systems of public transportation, and the density of our cities all transcend individual consumer choice. Changing these larger systems requires large-scale policy changes.

To solve the problems we face, we need to find ways to influence larger actors and transform institutional structures. If we want to keep our climate hospitable for human life, we need to look to accountability mechanisms that are likely to produce the sorts of large-scale and rapid changes needed. We need to look to entities to hold responsible that would have some real ability to stop the problem. Many of the world's climate campaigners have focused in recent years on holding national governments responsible.

One of the nice things about focusing on governments as the ones to hold responsible for climate change is that there are complex and functioning accountability mechanisms already set up at the national level. Governments can regulate car mileage requirements, they can invest in public transportation, they can set up smart electricity grids, and they can tax emissions.

The process of international meetings that began with the Kyoto Protocol in 1992, and led to the *United Nations Framework Convention on Climate Change* (UNFCCC) agreement in Paris in 2015, has been a major attempt to set up an accountability mechanism for climate change based on the notion that responsibility lies with national governments.

These meetings hold national governments responsible for the emissions that happen within their territories. At Paris, most of the nations of the world committed themselves to significant emissions reductions. That agreement was the result of years of work by campaigners to get nations to take on that responsibility.

These international meetings have had three of the five necessary elements for a functioning accountability mechanism: the problem has been voiced, it is seen as a moral, and not just practical imperative to resolve, and the responsibility has found a target in the national governments.

Much weaker has been the sanction side of this accountability mechanism. While many actors pushed at the Paris climate talks for an enforceable sanctions mechanism, none was agreed to. Instead of setting emissions limits that could be enforced by an international body with the power to impose sanctions, the Paris agreement simply has targets. To some observers this meant that the agreement was worthless. Others have argued that having made those agreements, each country is vulnerable to pressure from campaigners to keep to its agreements, or lose legitimacy, and risk being subject to pressure from other countries. These softer mechanisms are also sanctions and they do have impacts.

Whether or not the UNFCCC is an effective accountability mechanism will be based on the relative power of that soft sanctions mechanism, compared with the power that fossil fuel companies have to influence governments to not move toward strong emissions reducing policies. The next phase of the drama of climate change will largely be about the power side of the accountability mechanism that is the UNFCCC.

I have been active in the fossil fuel divestment movement. The movement argues that because of the tremendous political power the major fossil fuel companies hold, it is very difficult for national governments to regulate greenhouse gas emissions. These companies stand to lose trillions of dollars-worth of assets they already count on their books, if the reserves they own stay in the ground.[7] By asking colleges, towns, and pension funds to divest from fossil fuels, the movement has encouraged the public to see those companies as the ones responsible for the climate crisis. The divestment movement helps to give power to the national governments to keep to their commitments by undermining the power of those who will keep them from doing so. Once the companies are seen as pariahs, then it becomes harder for politicians to do their bidding.

Divestment can be seen as a part of the accountability mechanism being developed in the UNFCCC process. That process has a weak link in its lack of a direct way to make national governments follow through and act responsibly. The work done by these external actors to undermine the power that fossil fuel companies have over governments is a significant part of the accountability mechanism being set up by the UNFCCC. This is true, whether or not the negotiators saw it that way.

The movement to end the Dakota Access Pipeline in North Dakota was important for mobilizing a broad range of people to be climate activists, even as it ultimately failed to stop the oil from flowing. The movement drew tremendous attention to the role of fossil fuel infrastructure in the fight against clime change. One of the biggest challenges that fight has had is over the question of responsibility:

who to hold responsible for something dangerous that is woven into the way of life of most people on the planet.

Because the pipeline is a very expensive and long-lasting piece of infrastructure, built in a specific place, choosing it as a target helped make the diffuse problem of climate change very concrete. The movement to stop the pipeline was anchored at the Standing Rock Sioux reservation. In this case the people who are at the frontlines of climate destruction stood up for themselves and demanded a stop to an action that was not just bad for the climate but which endangered their way of life.

In terms of Young's categories, the people of the tribe have a strong interest and quite a bit of power. Interest, because the pipeline threatened the water that local lives depend on. And to the extent that they were in control of the land that the pipeline was to go through, they had quite a bit of power. On the other side, Energy Transfer Partners, the owner of the pipeline, was able to mobilize the resources of the state to arrest protestors and get the Army Corp of Engineers to permit the pipelines. Local protestors and their allies all around the country were able to use their privileged access to media, especially social media, to draw continued attention to the struggle.

The drama of the original protests gave values to the pipeline as wrong, because it meant investing long term in a technology that should be on its way out; it gave voice to that way of seeing the situation by engaging in dramatic and moving forms of protest; it parked the responsibility for a very complex and diffuse problem at the doorstep of Energy Transfer Partners and those funding it; the sanction was to not get that pipeline built, and to throw into question the economic value of any future planned pipelines; unfortunately with the election of Trump, the movement did not have the power to stop the pipeline.

Along with the local fight against the Dakota Access Pipeline there was a movement by outsiders to put pressure on banks to pull investments out of the project. Many people engaged in that action, as it was one thing that felt significant that outsiders were able to do. That process was not likely to stop the pipeline in its own, as any individual bank pulling out would not make capital for the project dry up. There were plenty of other banks to go in if one pulled out. But the anti-bank work was a way to keep the issue in the public's mind, as local actions against banks, all around the country, did get attention. Thus, that work was part of the voice side of the accountability mechanism, rather than the sanctions side, as many activists might have hoped.

With the fight against the pipeline, the power of transnational actors to get away with projects that are against human and environmental interests was challenged by people in one of the most marginalized communities in the country. And their ability to draw attention to the struggle was a victory for everyone interested in the long-term habitability of the planet. The power of large-scale fossil fuel producers can be challenged by any of us, and an end to the climate crisis will involve many of us finding targets to challenge and struggles to engage in. While the power of transnational actors is difficult for governments to control, grassroots power can be mobilized to hold that power to account. And while accountability failed in this case, many continue to draw inspiration and clarity from the attempt.

Economic Justice for Greece

The movement to elect Syriza to say "no" to the powerful institutions that insisted on imposing austerity on Greece, against the will of its people, had a powerful few months before it was crushed. The idea was that the people of Greece could shift the balance of power and claim sovereignty for the Greek people to have their government work in their interests.

The Greek people had a great interest in that change, and they engaged in powerful collective action to achieve their goals. One could imagine a supportive movement of people throughout the European Union, to use their privilege as outsiders to pressure the European institutions to relent and make the banks be the ones to take the loss for their bad investments. Unfortunately, in this case, that movement of solidarity was not strong enough to get the Troika of major powers (the European Commission [EC], the European Central Bank [ECB], and the International Monetary Fund [IMF]) that imposed the austerity on the Greeks to relent.

The Greek government had the choice to acquiesce to the Troika or leave the European Monetary Union. Some observers believe that the Syriza government capitulated unnecessarily and that transnational finance would have been dealt a significant blow if they had continued to say "no." Other observers believe that such a move would have been disastrous for the Greek people, and was a bad choice because it was not supported by the majority.

In analyzing the formation of power the Greek people faced, and the powers in the hands of each of the possible players in a strategy of accountability democracy, it is not clear that the Greek government had much power to enact a solution that would have served the people. The Greek people had some power over their national government, and they were the actors most interested in a change. And yet because of the rules of the European Monetary Union, the Greek people themselves did not have much power to enact a viable solution. The power in this case rested with the institutions of the European Union.

The Greek people, and the Syriza government, were successful at framing the problem as being caused by unscrupulous lending practices on the part of the banks and support for those practices on the part of the Troika. This framing of the issue resonated with many people in the international community. Unfortunately, that message of values did not become the dominant narrative in Northern Europe, where many continued to see the problem as caused by Greek irresponsibility. To those who accepted its analysis, Syriza, successfully parked the responsibility at the feet of the Troika. Unfortunately for the Greek people, that message was not spread strongly enough to Europe as a whole.

Where this attempt at accountability democracy fell short was in its ability to hold the Troika responsible. Perhaps they would have had the power to do that if they had been able to really mobilize Greek public opinion to be ready for an exit from the European Monetary Union, and together to deal with the very destabilizing consequences of such a choice. In this case, they would have made the Greek economy accountable to the people of Greece, and shifted the locus of the problem back to Greece.

Perhaps, if they had been able to convince large sectors of the populations of the Northern European countries of their values analysis, they might together have had the power to force a different decision from the Troika. A strong social justice movement in the rest of Europe might have made that possibility real.[8]

In this case, sovereignty did not rest in the government of Greece, but rather in the Troika. And those institutions are accountable to practically no one. Only a very strong movement across multiple European countries, specifically aimed at challenging the powers of the banks would be able to achieve that.

The Greek people have some power over their government, through relatively democratic elections. But an analysis of the configuration of power that they were facing would show that the Greek government would have had to have incredible support from the Greek population to say "no" to the banks and deal with the severe economic consequences of leaving the European Monetary

Union. The Greek people have power over their government, but the government didn't have the power to make the problem go away without incredible risk.

The failure of Syriza to end the crushing of living standards of the Greek people shows something important about accountability democracy: the way to a better world requires that we challenge power in all of its manifestations is a long and hard one. There is no quick solution to these problems. Rather what is required is a serious attention to the networks of power we inhabit; smart strategizing about what kinds of action will challenge power in lasting ways; a dogged commitment to continuing to think and rethink what kinds of action will make a difference; and an understanding of the deep structures that cause the problems that need to be held to account.

Conclusion

In approaching a social problem, it is important to look for each of the five elements of an accountability mechanism and to work to create systems of feedback between them. It is also important to follow Iris Marion Young's advice that we look at the "power, privilege, interest, and collective ability to make a difference" of each of the actors in any given scenario.

For any of us, no matter what our level of political knowledge or power, or how much time we have on our hands, there are ways we can use our capacities to disrupt the normal functioning of power relations and help reweave the social fabric in ways that hold power to account. The first step in any action is to stop and reflect on how that action might or might not help to build accountability democracy. Signing petitions being sent to someone with no ability to make a difference is not likely to be productive. For those with little time or expertise in understanding a social problem, it is important to look into who is doing something serious to deal with that problem and find ways to support their work.

For those working in nongovernmental organizations, it is important to analyze the matrix of power in which that work is embedded. Are you strengthening unaccountable powers even as you hold some local powers to account? These answers can never be definitive, but if you don't ask the question you are likely to be participating in things that are not in alignment with your values. For those working on making policy, the same rules apply. It is important to think holistically about the networks of power in which the policy operates, and what the likely outcomes are.

8

Acting Well in a Traumatized World

> *Regardless of the staggering dimensions of the world about us, the density of our ignorance, the risks of catastrophes to come, and our individual weakness within the immense collectivity, the fact remains that we are absolutely free today if we choose to will our existence in its finiteness, a finiteness which is open on the infinite. And in fact, any man [sic] who has known real loves, real revolts, real desires, and real will knows quite well that he has no need of any outside guarantee to be sure of his goals; their certitude comes from his own drive.*
>
> —SIMONE DE BEAUVOIR, *The Ethics of Ambiguity*[1]

Understanding the destructive powers that cause harm in our world, and living with our hearts open to the networks of connections in which we are embedded, allows us to see that every choice we make is wrapped up in the problems, and the solutions to those problems, endemic in our world. Living in a conscious relationship to the ways we are all connected lands us in a moral situation which is ambiguous, intellectually challenging, but which also can be somewhat freeing.

Many of us were raised with the belief that we could be moral people by following the Ten Commandments, the categorical imperative, or some other clear-cut set of rules. Those systems generally assume a world that is not in urgent need of change. They don't dig deeply enough into our responsibilities for creating and recreating the world through our actions. And so, those approaches to morality also leave us burdened by a sense that our lives are irrelevant to, and powerless in the face of, the wide-ranging traumas that connect us and permeate our world.

If we are all implicated in the creation and recreation of the social fabric we inhabit, and our responsibilities are not just for the acts we take that impact those living close to us in space and in time, then there is no clear set of rules to follow to allow us to be thoroughly moral in our work to repair our broken world. We don't discharge our moral responsibility by simply doing what society asks of us. Our responsibilities exceed our abilities to discharge them completely, and there is no unambiguous path to acting responsibly.

The task of living well, and responsibly, is intellectually challenging, because we are called upon to think about the nature of the systems of unjust power that structure our world, and what kinds of actions will hold those powers to account. At any given moment, there is an infinite number of possible things for us to do, and no clear rule book for what will be helpful. Knowing how to act on that responsibility requires an understanding of the systems of power we face, so that we can see the kinds of actions that will make a difference in solving those problems. Figuring out where best to put our energies and what kinds of things will make a significant difference require serious thought.

While this approach to morality is ambiguous and intellectually challenging, it can also be somewhat freeing. Our responsibilities are always greater than our abilities to make a difference. And so, it is a personal question how one will live well in such a fraught world. It is important to not burden oneself with a desire for moral purity or to work oneself to death trying to be good.

Many people living in our deeply unjust and interconnected world feel a sense of responsibility for the wrongs to which they are connected and try to be good people by looking for ways to be as pure as possible in their actions, trying as hard as they can to not have their lives touch the systems that cause harm to others or the environment. But a desire for purity will only encourage us to close our minds and hearts to the ugly things to which we are connected, because we cannot possible be pure in all of our choices. Rather than trying, and failing, to live pure individual lives, it is more useful, and more moral, to do what we can to make a difference.

Also, counterproductive is a way of living that is so responsible that it makes life miserable and in its misery dissuades others from taking up their responsibilities. Living a moral life means working to see as clearly as possible the operations of power that are damaging to ourselves, other people, and the environment. It requires us to take responsibility for our shared world. An ethics of social connection says that we are responsible for the wrongs which we have an ability to address. But that responsibility is not absolute.

Living morally means living with the weight of the world's problems on our shoulders, but not on them too heavily. It is important to attend to the reality of the kinds of impacts we can have, and to be realistic and mindful about that, and to make the best choices we can make to have a significant impact, while also inspiring others to take up those responsibilities. We need to not give ourselves a hard time for all of the ways that we burn carbon in our day to day activities, the ways we buy from a capitalist market, or the ways we participate in a commercial culture that is toxic. We also need to not give ourselves, or others a hard time for the ways we enjoy life, take care of ourselves, and relax. Feelings of guilt and shame are counterproductive to making a difference in the world. Being a martyr to one's causes generally makes one less effective than living with a strong ethic of self-care.

Most of the significant work that needs to be done to hold power to account takes place in social justice organizations. We need to do our best to support those organizations and movements. That can involve going to meetings and being active in organizations. But it can also involve speaking up in favor of what they are doing, shifting the attitudes of those around you, or engaging in smaller acts such as writing letters, following calls for boycotts, donating money, or voting smartly. On an individual level, it is up to each of us to work to understand the nature of the damaging powers we face and to figure out how best to make an impact given who we are, the constraints of our own lives, and the kinds of action that best fit our characters and life circumstances.

In order to address the crisis in accountability, we need to link our energies to others who are challenging the configurations of power that are damaging the world. We need to contest the powers embedded in national governments, and not allow the power that comes to be concentrated in states be used in unaccountable ways to dominate people. We need to develop accountability mechanisms that will limit the ability of large-scale agents, such as transnational corporations and transnational institutions, to destroy people's lives and the planet. We need to develop systems of meaning that inspire and help people to see themselves and others in ways that don't empower systems of domination. And we need to work to transform slippery configurations of power, such as markets, so that people can see the choices that enable chains of power to circulate in ways that appear as if no one were responsible for the damage they cause. All of those large tasks are made up of a wide variety of forms of action, some of them large and requiring significant commitments, and some of them very small and easy to do.

Building democracy means building the power of people to challenge the destructive configurations of power we face. It requires thinking of democracy as something more diffuse and closer to our lived experience than merely what happens in the circuits of governmental authority. While formal systems of democracy, such as representative democracy anchored in a state, authorize us as citizens with particular rights and responsibilities, accountability democracy requires our active work to challenge power in ways that no one authorizes us to do, and which existing social systems are largely set up to tell us we have no business doing. The roles we have as agents of accountability democracy are at least as ambiguous as the roles we have as moral agents when we understand morality according to a social connection model.

Working to build accountability democracy involves fighting for an expansion of the notion of rights, such that people can be seen as having rights to all of the things needed to live well, and it involves engaging in actions to hold people and institutions responsible for shaping the social fabric such that it is possible for those rights to be respected and those needs to be met.

Where there is law, those laws must be as accountable and fair as possible. When we think of punishment and sanction, we need to keep those dynamics within the framework of things done to get at the root causes of a problem as much as possible. When someone is held responsible for a problem, the focus should be less on punishing that person, and more on doing those things most likely to transform relations of power, such that the problem does not persist.

Building a better world means building accountability democracy wherever we can. It means understanding operations of destructive power, and looking to accountability mechanisms that can challenge and diffuse those powers. If we are to build systems that hold power to account, we need to look past notions of law and government, the rights and responsibilities of citizenship, and the requirements of individualist approaches to morality to legitimize our actions.

Instead we need to imagine a social world open before us that is shot through with relations of power, and where accountability mechanisms that challenge those forms of power exist and can be strengthened at all sorts of levels, from macro-scale fights against global trade deals, to everyday challenges to toxic systems of meaning.

The destructive powers we face can be challenged by accountability mechanisms which give voice to the problems they cause, put those cries of pain into a value-laden context such that they can be seen as a wrong to be righted, find someone to hold responsible so that there is a specific action that can be taken to disrupt the problem, create a sanction or disruption that will solve the problem, and ensure that whoever is engaging that sanction has the power to make a significant difference.

Conclusion

Living well in a traumatized world involves building our lives as agents of change, pacing ourselves, understanding how to be effective, not carrying our responsibilities in ways that make us unable to be effective, and holding power to account to the best of our abilities.

...

It is the job of each of us to be as mindful as we can be of the fabric of the social world we inhabit.

It is the job of each of us to heal ourselves from immobilizing guilt and shame.

We need to decolonize our minds from pro-capitalist ways of thinking that encourage us to see ourselves as autonomous individuals, and which erase our interconnections.

We need to stop thinking of market mechanisms as the best ways of changing the world.

We need to be brave and bold and not allow our thinking to be kept in small boxes that allow the power in our interconnections to go unchecked.

It is our job to pay attention to the ways that our senses of self are constructed through toxic discourses of individualism, dehumanization, consumerism, and cynicism.

We all need to work to develop accountability mechanisms where we can.

We all need to work to develop and use the concepts that will give meaning to, and make sense of, the pains that exist in this world.

We need to encourage ourselves and others to have the courage to do this work.

We need to encourage ourselves and others to challenge unaccountable power in ways that we can.

We need to focus on specific solvable problems, while also keeping in our sights the macrostructures that are causing the micro problems.

We need to fight macrostructures of power where we can.

We need to see ourselves as part of a global team, with different ones of us taking on different problems, while working as best as we can for synergy between our efforts. We need to use that sense of a team to calm our sense that we need to do everything all at once, and thereby burn out and not do much of anything.

We must be guard dogs who bark, and sometimes ones who bite, and at other times sly foxes who subvert.

We need to take risks and be brave and not shrink from challenging the entrenched powers that are killing us. The systems in which we live are not set up to encourage this. They are set up to encourage us to be nice and avoid conflict and be helpful to others, but never to challenge embedded systems of power.

We need to pace ourselves in this work, and not let a desire for purity burn us out and make us ineffective.

We need to adopt a posture of humility that allows us to be open to the possibilities for our limited capacities and our frailties.

We need to live in joy and create joy.

Notes

Introduction

1   This text, and all of the other text in the book which uses a different font, and does not have a citation attached to it, is fictional.

2   Money is perhaps the most important configuration of power in the contemporary world. It isn't dealt with in this text, because so much excellent work has been done on how money concentrates and deploys power. The best analysis of this remains: Karl Marx, *Economic and Philosophic Manuscripts of 1844,* trans. and ed. Martin Milligan (Mineola, NY: Dover Publications; New York: Dover Press, 2007). Bureaucracy is another important configuration of power not investigated here, is best dealt with by Max Weber, "Bureaucracy," in *From Max Weber: Essays in Sociology*, ed. H. H. Gerth and C. Wright Mills (London: Routledge Press, 2013), 196–244.

3   Paul Hawken, *Blessed Unrest: How the Largest Social Movement in History Is Restoring Grace, Justice, and Beauty to the World* (New York: Penguin Books, 2007), 2. Hawken makes a case, based on empirical study of the question, for the claim that there are over one million such organizations operating in the world at this time.

4   Jane Mayer, *Dark Money: The Hidden History of the Billionaires Behind the Rise of the Radical Right* (New York: Double Day, 2016), chapter 8.

5   Alexander Weheliye, *Habeas Viscus: Racializing Assemblages, Biopolitics, and Black Feminist Theories of the Human* (Durham, NC: Duke University Press, 2014).

6   Fred Block, *Capitalism: The Future of an Illusion* (Berkeley: University of California Press, 2018).

Chapter 1

1. This text, and all of the other text in the book which uses a different font, and does not have a citation attached to it, is fictional.

2. Juliane Reinecke and Jimmy Donaghey, "After Rana Plaza: Building Coalitional Power for Labor Rights between Unions and (Consumption Based) Social Movement Organizations," *Organization* 22 (5) (2015), 720–40, p. 720.

3. Jason Motlagh, "The Ghosts of Rana Plaza," accessed June 3, 2016, http://www.vqronline.org/issues/90/2/spring-2014

4. William Gomes, "Reason and Responsibility: The Rana Plaza Collapse," accessed May 21, 2017, https://www.opendemocracy.net/opensecurity/william-gomes/reason-and-responsibility-rana-plaza-collapse. May 9, 2013.

5. All definitions are from *The Shorter Oxford English Dictionary*, fourth edition (Oxford University Press, 1993).

6. Most writers on accountability focus on these two elements, and call them voice and sanction and sometimes bark and bite. Grant and Keohane claim that there are three main elements: standards, information, and sanction. See Ruth W. Grant and Robert O. Keohane, "Accountability and Abuses of Power in World Politics," *American Political Science Review* 99 (1), 29-44. In Chapter 6, I lay out five elements: values, voice, responsibility, power, and sanction. What they call as standards is similar to what I call as values.

7. Hans Jonas, *The Imperative of Responsibility: In Search of an Ethics for the Technological Age* (Chicago: University of Chicago Press, 1985), 5. Many ethical traditions have taken the implications of actions in the far-off distance into account. The most famous example of this is the Iroquois admonition to look at the implications of any actions on its impact on the seventh generation to follow. Still, Jonas is right that in the dominant Western traditions, ethics is seen as being about actions that are proximate in time and space.

Chapter 2

1. This text, and all of the other text in the book which uses a different font, and does not have a citation attached to it, is fictional.

2 John Locke, *Two Treatises of Government* (New York: Random House, 1993), 119.

3 Ibid., paraphrased from 129–41.

4 Ibid., 125.

5 Ronald Reagan, Speech at the Republican National Convention, Platform Committee Meeting, Miami, FL, July 31, 1968.

6 Joseph Koterski, "Introduction to Karl Jaspers," *The Question of German Guilt,* trans E. B. Ashton (Fordham, NY: Fordham University Press, 2001), xxii.

7 Michael Onyebuchi Eze, *Intellectual History in Contemporary South Africa* (New York: Macmillan Press, 2010), 190–91.

8 Segun Gbadegesin, "Yoruba Philosophy: Individuality, Community, and the Moral Order," in *African Philosophy: An Anthology*, ed. Emmanuel Chukwudi Eze (Lynchburg, VA: Blackwell Press, 1998), 133.

9 Immanuel Kant, *Grounding for the Metaphysic of Morals with On a Supposed Right to Lie Because of Philanthropic Concerns,* third ed., trans. Jams Ellington (Cambridge, MA: Hackett Publishing Company).

10 Helga Varden, "Kant and Lying to the Murderer at the Door . . . One More Time: Kant's Legal Philosophy and Lies to Murderers and Nazis," *Journal of Social Philosophy* 41 (4) (2010), 403–21, p. 418.

11 Aimé Césaire, *Discourse on Colonialism,* trans. Joan Pinkham (New York: Monthly Review Press, 1972), 1–2.

12 Iris Marion Young, "Responsibility and Global Justice: A Social Connection Model," *Social Philosophy and Policy* 23 (1) (2006), 102–30.

13 Ibid., 119.

14 Ibid., 119–23.

15 Ibid., 125.

16 Ibid., 127.

17 Ibid., 128.

18 Ibid.

19 Ibid., 129.

20 James Baldwin, "The White Man's Guilt," *James Baldwin: Collected Essays. Volume 1* (New York: Library of America, 1965), 722–27, p. 723.

21 Karl Jaspers, *The Question of German Guilt,* trans. E. B. Ashton (Fordham and New York: Fordham University Press, 2001).

22 Ibid., 63–4.

23 Ibid., 115.

24 Ibid., 28.

25 Ibid., 26.

26 Ibid., 30.

27 Simone de Beauvoir, *The Ethics of Ambiguity,* trans. Bernard Frechtman (New York: Citadel Press, 1962), 16.

28 Iris Marion Young, "Responsibility and Global Justice: A Social Connection Model," *Social Philosophy and Policy* 23 (1), 102–30, p. 122.

29 Anthony F. Lang, Jr., "Punishing Genocide: A Critical Reading of the International Court of Justice," in *Accountability for Collective Wrongdoing,* ed. Tracy Isaacs and Richard Vernon (Cambridge, UK: Cambridge University Press, 2011), 110–12.

Chapter 3

1 This text, and all of the other text in the book which uses a different font and does not have a citation attached to it, is fictional.

2 Yascha Mounk, *The People vs. Democracy: Why Our Freedom Is in Danger and How to Save It* (Cambridge, MA: Harvard University Press, 2018), 5.

3 Ibid., 135.

4 Ibid., 174.

5 Fareed Zakaria, "The Rise of Illiberal Democracy," *Foreign Affairs* 76 (1997), 22–43.

6 Robert Kuttner, *Can Democracy Survive Global Capitalism?* (New York: W.W. Norton & Company, 2018), 299.

7 Colin Crouch, *Post-Democracy* (Cambridge UK: Polity Press, 2004), 4.

8 Wolfgang Streek, *Buying Time: The Delayed Crisis of Democratic Capitalism,* trans. Patrick Camiller and David Fernbach (New York: Verso, 2017); Yanis

Varoufakis, *Adults in the Room; My Battle with the European and American Deep Establishment* (New York: Farrar, Straus, Giroux, 2017).

9   Kuttner, *Can Democracy Survive Global Capitalism?*, xxi.

10   Ibid., xx.

11   Moisés Naím, *The End of Power: From Boardrooms to Battlefields and Churches to States: Why Being in Charge Isn't What It Used to Be* (New York: Basic Books, 2014), 58.

12   See Helena Sheehan, *Syriza Wave: Surging and Crashing with the Greek Left* (New York: New York University Press, 2017), for a description of that time within the Greek left, which largely argues that Tsipras could and should have chosen to default. See Varoufakis, *Adults in the Room*, for a blow by blow insider's account of how it all happened.

13   I use the term "capitalist processes" rather than the more common "capitalist system," because the metaphor of a system encourages us to think of capitalism as something working like a machine which must be destroyed all at once or not at all. In my *Getting Past Capitalism: History, Vision, Hope,* I argue that is it better to see capitalism as a set of practices which can be interrupted through a variety of forms of action. Cynthia Kaufman, *Getting Past Capitalism: History, Vision, Hope* (Landham, MD: Lexington Books, 2012).

14   Kuttner, *Can Democracy Survive Global Capitalism?*.

15   Jan Nederveen Pieterse, *Multipolar Globalization: Emerging Economies and Development* (New York: Routledge, 2017), 14.

16   Pieterse, *Multipolar Globalization,* 14.

17   Karl Marx and Friedrich Engels, "The Communist Manifesto," *Marx-Engels Reader,* ed. Robert C. Tucker (New York: W.W. Norton, 1978), 476.

Chapter 4

1   This text, and all of the other text in the book which uses a different font, and does not have a citation attached to it, is fictional.

2   Wendy Brown, *Undoing the Demos: Neoliberalism's Stealth Revolution* (Cambridge, MA: Massachusetts Institute of Technology Press, 2015), 91.

3 Philip Pettit, *Republicanism: A Theory of Freedom and Government* (Oxford: Oxford University Press, 1999), 20.

4 This is not to argue that Hamilton was everything that a social justice advocate would want him to be. His financial policies were largely in the interest of those with capital. The point being made here is that Hamilton, and the republican tradition of which he was a part, have something to offer us in thinking about the nature of government, and that the ways that the liberal tradition of Jefferson undermines attention to the development of accountable system of government is worth challenging.

5 Terry Bouton, *Taming Democracy: "The People," The Founders, and the Troubled Ending of the American Revolution* (Oxford: Oxford University Press, 2009).

6 Ron Chernow, *Alexander Hamilton* (New York: Penguin Books, 2016), 629.

7 Pettit, *Republicanism*, viii.

8 Ibid., 210.

9 Ibid., 9.

10 Michael Schudson, *The Good Citizen: A History of American Civic Life* (New York: Free Press, 2011), 8–9.

11 Ibid., 9.

12 This shift was marked in the 1970s by feminists who declared that "the personal is the political." As women advocated for a shift in the relations of power between men and women, they were routinely criticized by men for focusing on trivial, personal issues as opposed to political ones, such as opposing the war in Viet Nam.

13 Schudson, *The Good Citizen*, 310–11.

14 John Keane, *The Life and Death of Democracy* (New York: W.W. Norton & Company, 2009), xxvii.

15 John Keane, "Brace Yourselves as Democracy Reshapes Itself." *The Sydney Morning Herald,* November 21, 2008, accessed February 28, 2017, http://www.johnkeane.net/brace-yourselves-as-democracy-reshapes-itself/ 4/17/16

16 Keane, *The Life and Death of Democracy*, 736.

17 Pierre Rosanvallon, *Counter-Democracy: Politics in an Age of Distrust*, trans. Arthur Goldhammer (Cambridge, UK: Cambridge University Press, 2013), 8.

18 Ibid., 19.

19 Aristotle, *Politics*. In the Basic Works of Aristotle, ed. Richard McKeon (New York: Random House, 1941), Book 1, Chapter 2, 1130.

20 Brown, *Undoing the Demos*, 95.

21 Benedict Anderson, *Imagined Communities: Reflections on the Origin and Spread of Nationalism* (London: Verso Press, 2016).

22 Brown, *Undoing the Demos,* Chapter 6, 175.

23 Martha Nussbaum, *Cultivating Humanity: A Classical Defense of Reform in Liberal Education* (Cambridge, MA: Harvard University Press, 1998), 10.

24 April Carter, *The Political Theory of Global Citizenship* (New York: Routledge, 2006), 168.

25 Ian Shapiro, "Collusion in Restraint of Democracy: Against Political Deliberation," *Daedalus* 146 (3) (Summer 2017), 77–84, p. 77.

26 Ibid., 83.

27 Xavier de Souza Briggs, *Democracy as Problem Solving: Civic Capacity in Communities Across the Globe* (Cambridge, MA: Massachusetts Institute of Technology Press, 2008), 31–32.

28 Crouch, *Post-Democracy*, 15.

29 Ibid., 111.

30 John Holloway, *Change the World Without Taking Power: The Meaning of Revolution Today* (London: Pluto Press, 2005).

Chapter 5

1 This text, and all of the other text in the book which uses a different font, and does not have a citation attached to it, is fictional.

2 Gianfranco Poggi, *Forms of Power* (Cambridge, UK: Polity Press, 2001), 8. For a similar and very widely influential approach to power, see Steven Lukes, *Power: A Radical View*, second ed. (New York: Palgrave Press, 2007).

3 Martin Luther King, Jr., *Where Do We Go from Here: Chaos or Community* (New York: Harper and Row Publishers, 1967), 37.

4 Michel Foucault, *The History of Sexuality*, trans. Robert Hurley (New York: Random House, 1980), 92–93.

5 Gilles Deleuze and Félix Guattari, *A Thousand Plateaus,* trans. Brian Massumi (Minneapolis, MN: University of Minnesota Press, 1987).

6 Jessica T. Mathews, "Power Shift," *Foreign Affairs* 76 (1997), 50–66, p. 50.

7 Jeffrey A. Hart and Aseem Prakash, *Globalization and Governance* (New York: Routledge Press, 2003), 161.

8 Antonio Gramsci, "Philosophy, Common Sense, Language and Folklore," in *The Antonio Gramsci Reader,* ed. and trans. David Forgacs (New York: New York University Press, 2000), 323–62.

9 Andreas Schedler, "Conceptualizing Accountability," in *The Self-Restraining State: Power and Accountability in New Democracies,* ed. Andreas Schedler, Larry Diamond, and Marc F. Plattner (Boulder, CO: Lynne Rienner Publishers, 1999), 18–19.

10 Ibid., 9–20.

11 Michael Omi and Howard Winant, *Racial Formation in the United States from the 1960s to the 1990s* (New York: Routledge, 2015), 114.

12 Stuart Hall, "New Ethnicities," *Stuart Hall: Critical Dialogues in Cultural Studies* (1996), 441–49, p. 444.

13 Shapiro, *The State of Democratic Theory*, 50.

14 Ibid., 51.

15 Nicos Poulantzas, *State, Power, Socialism,* trans. Patrick Camiller (London: Verso Press, 2014).

16 #BlackLivesMatter was launched in response to the murder of Trayvon Martin by vigilante George Zimmerman and yet the subsequent movement had focused mostly on police killings.

17 Patricia Williams, *The Alchemy of Race and Rights: Diary of a Law Professor* (Cambridge, MA: Harvard University Press, 1992), 159.

18 Cheryl Harris, "Whiteness as Property," *Harvard Law Review* (1993), 1707–91, p. 1716.

19 Sylvia Wynter, "Unsettling the Coloniality of Being/Power/Truth/Freedom: Towards the Human after Man, Its Overrepresentation—An Argument," *The New Centennial Review* 3 (3) (Fall 2003), 257–337, p. 291.

20 Sylvia Wynter, "On How We Mistook the Map for the Territory, and Reimprisoned Ourselves in Our Unbearable Wrongness of Being, of

Desêtre: Black Studies Toward the Human Project," in *Not Only the Master's Tools: African-American Studies in Theory and Practice*, ed. Lewis Ricardo Gordon and Jane Anna Gordon (New York: Paradigm Press, 2006), 107–69, p. 118.

21 Weheliye, *Habeas Viscus*, 3.

22 Michele Foucault, *Discipline and Punish: The Birth of the Prison*, trans. Alan Sheridan (New York: Vintage Press, 1995).

23 Gilles Deleuze and Félix Guattari, *Anti-Oedipus: Capitalism and Schizophrenia*, trans. Robert Hurley, Mark Seem, and Helen R. Lane (New York: Vintage Press, 1977).

24 Erich Fromm, *The Art of Loving* (New York: Harper Press, 2006) 3.

25 Richard Layard, *Happiness: Lessons from a New Science* (New York: Penguin Press, 2006).

26 For an analysis of the elements that go into making a powerful social movement, see Bill Moyer, *Doing Democracy: The MAAP Model for Organizing Social Movements* (Gabriola Island, BC: New Society Publishers, 2001).

27 Adam Smith, *The Theory of Moral Sentiments* (New York: Penguin Books, 2010).

28 Karl Polanyi, *The Great Transformation: The Political and Economic Origins of Our Time* (Boston: Beacon Press, 2001).

29 Fred Block and Margaret Sommers, *The Power of Market Fundamentalism: Karl Polanyi's Critique* (Cambridge, MA: Harvard University Press, 2014), 20–21. See also Kate Raworth, *Doughnut Economics: 7 Ways to Think Like a 21st-Century Economist* (White River Junction, VT: Chelsea Green Publishing, 2017) 71.

30 For an argument for a whole different approach to economics based on finding the sweet spot in the doughnut between, on the inside of the doughnut, lives of impoverishment, and on the outside of the doughnut processes that exceed the environment's capacities, see Raworth, *Doughnut Economics*.

31 Antonio Gramsci, "War of Position War of Maneuver," in *The Antonio Gramsci Reader*, ed. and trans. David Forgacs (New York: New York University Press, 2000), 222–45.

32 Poulantzas, *State, Power, Socialism*, 265.

33 Fredrik Galtung and Jeremy Pope, "The Global Coalition Against Corruption: Evaluating Transparency International," in *The Self-Restraining State: Power and Accountability in New Democracies*, ed. Andreas Schedler, Larry Diamond, and Marc F. Plattner (Boulder, CO: Lynne Rienner Publishers, 1999).

34 Ibid., 270.

35 Ibid., 263.

36 Transparency International, accessed July 17, 2017, https://www.transparency.org/research/bpi/bpi

37 Williams, *The Alchemy of Race and Rights*.

Chapter 6

1 Young, "Responsibility and Global Justice," 102–30, p. 127.

2 Incite! *The Revolution Will Not Be Funded: Beyond the Non-profit Industrial Complex* (Durham, NC: Duke University Press, 2017).

3 Diane Ravitch, *The Death and Life of the Great American School System: How Testing and Choice Are Undermining Education* (New York: Basic Books, 2016).

4 Kerry Patterson, Joseph Grenny, Ron McMillan, Al Switzler, and David Maxfield, *Crucial Accountability: Tools for Resolving Violated Expectations, Broken Commitments, and Bad Behavior*, Second ed. (New York: McGraw-Hill, 2013), 39.

5 Jennifer Rubenstein, "Accountability in an Unequal World," *The Journal of Politics* 69 (3) (August 2007), 616–23. This section draws heavily on Rubenstein's work, but categorizes the types of sanction differently.

6 Rebecca Gordon, *American Nuremberg: The U.S. Officials Who Should Stand Trial for Post-9/11 War Crimes* (New York: Hot Books Publishing, 2016).

7 Michael Hanemann, "How California Came to Pass AB 32, the Global Warming Solutions Act of 2006," IDEAS Working Paper Series from RePEc, 2007.

8 Rainer Braun and Judy Gearhat, "Who Should Code Your Conduct? Trade Union and NGO Differences in the Fight for Workers' Rights," *Development*

in Practice 14 (1–2) (2004), 183–96; Ronnie Lipschutz, "Sweating It Out: NGO Campaigns and Trade Union Empowerment," *Development in Practice*, 14 (1–2) (2004), 197–209.

9 Ramón Feenstra and Andreu Casero-Ripollés, "Democracy in the Digital Communication Environment: A Typology Proposal of Political Monitoring Processes," *International Journal of Communication* 8 (2014), 2448–68, p. 2448.

10 Ibid., 2460.

11 Frances Fox Piven and Richard Cloward, *Poor People's Movements: Why They Succeed, How They Fail* (New York: Vintage Books, 1978).

12 Streek, *Buying Time*; Varoufakis, *Adults in the Room*.

13 Keane, *The Life and Death of Democracy*, 734.

14 Joel Feinberg, *Rights, Justice, and the Bounds of Liberty: Essays in Social Philosophy* (Princeton, NJ: Princeton University Press, 1980), 153.

15 Ibid., 153.

16 William T. Armaline, Davita Silfen Glasberg, and Bandana Purkayastha, *The Human Rights Enterprise* (London: Polity Press, 2015), 14.

17 Patterson, Grenny, McMillan, Al Switzler, and Maxfield, *Crucial Accountability*.

18 Thomas Goetz, "Harnessing the Power of Feedback Loops," *Wired Magazine*, June 19, 2011.

19 Ibid., n.p.

20 Kaufman, *Getting Past Capitalism: History, Vision, Hope*.

Chapter 7

1 This text, and all of the other text in the book which uses a different font, and does not have a citation attached to it, is fictional.

2 Timoci Naulusala, Age 7. Speech to the COP 23 Meeting in Bonn. November 15, 2017. In PMC Editor, Timoci shares his story of climate change—it's real and urgent. Asia Pacific Report, accessed November 20,

2019, https://asiapacificreport.nz/2017/11/16/timoci-shares-his-story-of-climate-change-its-real-and-urgent/

3 Young, "Responsibility and Global Justice," 102–30, p. 127.
4 Reinecke and Donaghey, "After Rana Plaza: Building Coalitional Power for Labor Rights Between Unions and (Consumption Based) Social Movement Organizations," 720–40, p. 725.
5 Change the NYPD, accessed August 2019, http://changethenypd.org/community-safety-act
6 Mayer, *Dark Money*.
7 Bill McKibben, "Global Warming's Terrifying New Math," *Rolling Stone* 19 (7) (2012), 2012.
8 For an attempt to develop that movement, see: Democracy in Europe Movement 2025, accessed July 30, 2018, https://diem25.org/

Chapter 8

1 de Beauvoir, *The Ethics of Ambiguity*, 159.

Bibliography

Anderson, Benedict. *Imagined Communities: Reflections on the Origin and Spread of Nationalism*. London: Verso Press, 2016.

Aristotle. *Politics*. In the Basic Works of Aristotle, ed. Richard McKeon. New York: Random House, 1941.

Armaline, William T., Davita Silfen Glasberg, and Bandana Purkayastha. *The Human Rights Enterprise*. London: Polity Press, 2015.

Baldwin, James. "The White Man's Guilt." *James Baldwin: Collected Essays. Volume 1*. New York: Library of America, 1965, 722–27.

Block, Fred. *Capitalism: The Future of an Illusion*. Berkeley: University of California Press, 2018.

Block, Fred, and Margaret Sommers. *The Power of Market Fundamentalism: Karl Polanyi's Critique*. Cambridge, MA: Harvard University Press, 2014.

Bouton, Terry. *Taming Democracy: "The People," the Founders, and the Troubled Ending of the American Revolution*. Oxford: Oxford University Press, 2009.

Braun, Rainer, and Judy Gearhat. "Who Should Code Your Conduct? Trade Union and NGO Differences in the Fight for Workers' Rights." *Development in Practice*, 14 (1–2) (2004), 183–96.

Briggs, Xavier de Souza. *Democracy as Problem Solving: Civic Capacity in Communities Across the Globe*. Cambridge, MA: Massachusetts Institute of Technology Press, 2008.

Brown, Wendy. *Undoing the Demos: Neoliberalism's Stealth Revolution*. Cambridge, MA: Massachusetts Institute of Technology Press, 2015.

Carter, April. *The Political Theory of Global Citizenship*. New York: Routledge, 2006.

Césaire, Aimé. *Discourse on Colonialism*, trans. Joan Pinkham. New York: Monthly Review Press, 1972.

Change the NYPD, accessed August 2019, http://changethenypd.org/community-safety-act.

Chernow, Ron. *Alexander Hamilton*. New York: Penguin Books, 2016.

Crouch, Colin. *Post-Democracy*. Cambridge, UK: Polity Press, 2004.

de Beauvoir, Simone. *The Ethics of Ambiguity*, trans. Bernard Frechtman. New York: Citadel Press, 1962.

Deleuze, Gilles, and Félix Guattari. *Anti-Oedipus: Capitalism and Schizophrenia*, trans. Robert Hurley, Mark Seem, and Helen R. Lane. New York: Vintage Press, 1977.

Deleuze, Gilles, and Félix Guattari A. *Thousand Plateaus*, trans. Brian Massumi. Minneapolis, MN: University of Minnesota Press, 1987.

Democracy in Europe Movement 2025, accessed July 30, 2018, https://diem25.org/.

Eze, Michael Onyebuchi. *Intellectual History in Contemporary South Africa*. New York: Macmillan Press, 2010, 190–91.

Feenstra, Ramón, and Andreu Casero-Ripollés. "Democracy in the Digital Communication Environment: A Typology Proposal of Political Monitoring Processes." *International Journal of Communication*, 8 (2014), 2448–68, p. 2448.

Feinberg, Joel. *Rights, Justice, and the Bounds of Liberty: Essays in Social Philosophy*. Princeton, NJ: Princeton University Press, 1980.

Foucault, Michel. *Discipline and Punish: The Birth of the Prison*, trans. Alan Sheridan. New York: Vintage Press, 1995.

Foucault, Michel. *The History of Sexuality*, trans. Robert Hurley. New York: Random House, 1980.

Fromm, Erich. *The Art of Loving*. New York: Harper Press, 2006.

Galtung, Fredrik, and Jeremy Pope. "The Global Coalition Against Corruption: Evaluating Transparency International." In *The Self-Restraining State: Power and Accountability in New Democracies*, ed. Andreas Schedler, Larry Diamond, and Marc F. Plattner. Boulder, CO: Lynne Rienner Publishers, 1999.

Gbadegesin, Segun. "Yoruba Philosophy: Individuality, Community, and the Moral Order." In *African Philosophy: An Anthology*, ed. Emmanuel Chukwudi Eze. Lynchburg, VA: Blackwell Press, 1998.

Goetz, Thomas. "Harnessing the Power of Feedback Loops." *Wired Magazine*, June 19, 2011.

Gomes, William. "Reason and Responsibility: The Rana Plaza Collapse," accessed May 21, 2017, https://www.opendemocracy.net/opensecurity/william-gomes/reason-and-responsibility-rana-plaza-collapse, May 9, 2013.

Gramsci, Antonio. "Philosophy, Common Sense, Language and Folklore." In *The Antonio Gramsci Reader*, ed. and trans. David Forgacs. New York: New York University Press, 2000.

Gramsci, Antonio. "War of Position War of Maneuver." In *The Antonio Gramsci Reader*, ed. and trans. David Forgacs. New York: New York University Press, 2000.

Grant, Ruth W., and Robert O. Keohane. "Accountability and Abuses of Power in World Politics." *American Political Science Review* 99 (1), 29–44.

Gordon, Rebecca. *American Nuremberg: The U.S. Officials Who Should Stand Trial for Post-9/11 War Crimes*. New York: Hot Books Publishing, 2016.

Hanemann, Michael. "How California Came to Pass AB 32, the Global Warming Solutions Act of 2006." IDEAS Working Paper Series from RePEc, 2007.

Hall, Stuart. "New Ethnicities." In *Stuart Hall: Critical Dialogues in Cultural Studies*. New York: Routledge, 1996.

Harris, Cheryl. "Whiteness as Property." *Harvard Law Review* (1993), 1707–91.

Hart, Jeffrey A. Hart, and Aseem Prakash. *Globalization and Governance*. New York: Routledge Press, 2003.

Hawken, Paul. *Blessed Unrest: How the Largest Social Movement in History Is Restoring Grace, Justice, and Beauty to the World*. New York: Penguin Books, 2007.

Holloway, John. *Change the World Without Taking Power: The Meaning of Revolution Today*. London: Pluto Press, 2005.

Incite! *The Revolution Will Not Be Funded: Beyond the Non-Profit Industrial Complex*. Durham, NC: Duke University Press 2017.

Jaspers, Karl. *The Question of German Guilt*, trans. E. B. Ashton. Fordham, NY: Fordham University Press, 2001.

Jonas, Hans. *The Imperative of Responsibility: In Search of an Ethics for the Technological Age*. Chicago: University of Chicago Press, 1985.

Kant, Immanuel. *Grounding for the Metaphysic of Morals with on a Supposed Right to Live Because of Philanthropic Concerns*, trans. Jams Ellington, third ed. Cambridge, MA: Hackett Publishing Company.

Kaufman, Cynthia. *Getting Past Capitalism: History, Vision, Hope*. Landham, MD: Lexington Books, 2012.

Keane, John. "Brace Yourselves as Democracy Reshapes Itself." *The Sydney Morning Herald*, November 21, 2008, accessed February 28, 2017, http://www.johnkeane.net/brace-yourselves-as-democracy-reshapes-itself/ 4/17/16.

Keane, John. *The Life and Death of Democracy*. New York: W.W. Norton & Company, 2009.

King, Martin Luther, Jr. *Where Do We Go from Here: Chaos or Community*. New York: Harper and Row Publishers, 1967.

Koterski, Joseph. "Introduction to Karl Jaspers." *The Question of German Guilt*, trans. E. B. Ashton. Fordham, NY: Fordham University Press, 2001.

Kuttner, Robert. *Can Democracy Survive Global Capitalism?* New York: W.W. Norton & Company, 2018.

Lang, Anthony F., Jr. "Punishing Genocide: A Critical Reading of the International Court of Justice." In *Accountability for Collective Wrongdoing*, ed. Tracy Isaacs and Richard Vernon. Cambridge, UK: Cambridge University Press, 2011.

Layard, Richard. *Happiness: Lessons from a New Science*. New York: Penguin Press, 2006.

Lipschutz, Ronnie. "Sweating It Out: NGO Campaigns and Trade Union Empowerment." *Development in Practice* 14 (1–2) (2004), 197–209.

Locke, John. *Two Treatises of Government*. New York: Random House, 1993.

Lukes, Steven. *Power: A Radical View*, second ed. New York: Palgrave Press, 2007.

Marx, Karl. *Economic and Philosophic Manuscripts of 1844*, trans. and ed. Martin Milligan. Mineola, NY: Dover Publications, 2007.

Marx, Karl, and Friedrich Engels. "The Communist Manifesto." In *Marx-Engels Reader*, ed. Robert C. Tucker. New York: W.W. Norton, 1978.

Mathews, Jessica T. "Power Shift." *Foreign Affairs* 76 (1997), 50–66.

Mayer, Jane. *Dark Money: The Hidden History of the Billionaires Behind the Rise of the Radical Right*. New York: Double Day, 2016.

McKibben, Bill. "Global Warming's Terrifying New Math." *Rolling Stone* 19 (7) (2012), 2012.

Motlaugh, Jason. "The Ghosts of Rana Plaza," accessed June 3, 2016, http://www.vqronline.org/issues/90/2/spring-2014.

Mounk, Yascha. *The People vs. Democracy: Why Our Freedom Is in Danger and How to Save It*. Cambridge, MA: Harvard University Press, 2018.

Moyer, Bill. *Doing Democracy: The MAAP Model for Organizing Social Movements*. Gabriola Island, BC: New Society Publishers, 2001.

Naím, Moisés. *The End of Power: From Boardrooms to Battlefields and Churches to States: Why Being in Charge Isn't What It Used to Be*. New York: Basic Books, 2014.

Nussbaum, Martha. *Cultivating Humanity: A Classical Defense of Reform in Liberal Education*. Cambridge, MA: Harvard University Press, 1998.

Omi, Michael, and Howard Winant. *Racial Formation in the United States from the 1960s to the 1990s*. New York: Routledge Press, 2015.

Oxford English Dictionary, shorter, fourth edition. Oxford University Press, 1993.

Patterson, Kerry, Joseph Grenny, Ron McMillan, Al Switzler, and David Maxfield. *Crucial Accountability: Tools for Resolving Violated Expectations, Broken Commitments, and Bad Behavior*, Second ed. New York: McGraw-Hill, 2013.

Pettit, Philip. *Republicanism: A Theory of Freedom and Government*. Oxford: Oxford University Press, 1999.

Pieterse, Jan Nederveen. *Multipolar Globalization: Emerging Economies and Development*. New York: Routledge, 2017.
Poggi, Gianfranco. *Forms of Power*. Cambridge, UK: Polity Press, 2001.
Polanyi, Karl. *The Great Transformation: The Political and Economic Origins of Our Time*. Boston: Beacon Press, 2001.
Poulantzas, Nicos. *State, Power, Socialism*, trans. Patrick Camiller. London: Verso Press, 2014.
Ravitch, Diane. *The Death and Life of the Great American School System: How Ting and Choice Are Undermining Education*. New York: Basic Books, 2016.
Raworth, Kate. *Doughnut Economics: 7 Ways to Think Like a 21st-Century Economist*. White River Junction, VT: Chelsea Green Publishing, 2017.
Reagan, Ronald. Speech at the Republican National Convention, Platform Committee Meeting, Miami, FL, July 31, 1968.
Reinecke, Juliane Reinecke, and Jimmy Donaghey. "After Rana Plaza: Building Coalitional Power for Labor Rights Between Unions and (Consumption Based) Social Movement Organizations." *Organization* 22 (5) (2015), 720–40.
Rosanvallon, Pierre. *Counter-Democracy: Politics in an Age of Distrust*, trans. Arthur Goldhammer. Cambridge, UK: Cambridge University Press, 2013.
Rubenstein, Jennifer Rubenstein. "Accountability in an Unequal World." *The Journal of Politics* 69 (3) (August 2007), 616–23.
Schedler, Andreas. "Conceptualizing Accountability." In *The Self-Restraining State: Power and Accountability in New Democracies*, ed. Andreas Schedler, Larry Diamond, and Marc F. Plattner. Boulder, CO: Lynne Rienner Publishers, 1999.
Schudson, Michael. *The Good Citizen: A History of American Civic Life*. New York: Free Press, 2011.
Shapiro, Ian. "Collusion in Restraint of Democracy: Against Political Deliberation." *Daedalus*, 146 (3) (Summer 2017), 77–84.
Shapiro, Ian. *The State of Democratic Theory*. Princeton, NJ: Princeton University Press, 2009.
Sheehan, Helena. *Syriza Wave: Surging and Crashing with the Greek Left*. New York: New York University Press, 2017.
Smith, Adam. *The Theory of Moral Sentiments*. New York: Penguin Books, 2010.
Streek, Wolfgang. *Buying Time: The Delayed Crisis of Democratic Capitalism*, trans. Patrick Camiller and David Fernbach. New York: Verso, 2017.
Transparency International, accessed July 17, 2017, https://www.transparency.org/research/bpi/bpi
Varden, Helga. "Kant and Lying to the Murderer at the Door . . . One More Time: Kant's Legal Philosophy and Lies to Murderers and Nazis." *Journal of Social Philosophy* 41 (4) (2010), 403–21.

Varoufakis, Yanis. *Adults in the Room; My Battle with the European and American Deep Establishment*. New York: Farrar, Straus, Giroux, 2017.
Weber, Max. "Bureaucracy." In *From Max Weber: Essays in Sociology*, ed. H. H. Gerth and C. Wright Mills. London: Routledge, 2013.
Weheliye, Alexander. *Habeas Viscus: Racializing Assemblages, Biopolitics, and Black Feminist Theories of the Human*. Durham, NC: Duke University Press, 2014.
Williams, Patricia. *The Alchemy of Race and Rights: Diary of a Law Professor*. Cambridge, MA: Harvard University Press, 1992.
Wynter, Sylvia. "On How We Mistook the Map for the Territory, and Reimprisoned Ourselves in Our Unbearable Wrongness of Being, of Desêtre: Black Studies Toward the Human Project." In *Not Only the Master's Tools: African-American Studies in Theory and Practice*, ed. Lewis Ricardo Gordon and Jane Anna Gordon. New York: Paradigm Press, 2006.
Wynter, Sylvia. "Unsettling the Coloniality of Being/Power/Truth/Freedom: Towards the Human after Man, Its Overrepresentation—An Argument." *The New Centennial Review* 3 (3) (Fall 2003), 257–337.
Young, Iris Marion. "Responsibility and Global Justice: A Social Connection Model." *Social Philosophy and Policy* 23 (1), 102–30.
Zakaria, Fareed. "The Rise of Illiberal Democracy." *Foreign Affairs* 76 (1997), 22–43.

Index

AB 32, climate regulation   141
Accord for Fire and Building Safety in Bangladesh   167
accountability   16, 40, 127–38, 158–62
   for climate crisis   174–80
   crisis of   3–4, 7–8, 16, 40, 103–4
   democracy   7–8, 10, 12, 18–20, 32, 80–5, 93, 129, 163–84
      building   163–84, 189–90
      citizenship for   91
      education for   88
      ethics of   35–58
   feedback loops   151–6
   of governments   107–11, 130
   liberal   7
   mechanisms   8, 11–12, 18–20, 28–9, 32, 129–31
      power   4–5, 7–8, 15, 19, 134–5
      responsibility   8, 18–19, 132–4
      sanction   8, 15, 18–20, 137–51, 194 n.6
      values   8, 14, 18, 115, 131–2
      voice   8, 14, 18, 115, 135–7, 194 n.6
   political   103–4
   pro-capitalist thought   153–6
   for Rana Plaza disaster   29–33
   for reform and revolution   156–8
   social welfare systems and   5
   as tool   4–5
American Nuremberg (Gordon)   139
Anarchism   109–10
Anderson, Benedict   87
Aristotle   41, 75, 86
Armaline, William T.   150
Art of Loving, The (Fromm)   116

Baldwin, James   51
bio-power   116
#BlackLivesMatter   113, 145, 171, 200 n.16
Block, Fred   120
Boko Haram   143
brain circulation   65–6
brain drain   65–6
Bribe Payers Index   124
Briggs, Xavier De Souza   90
"Bring Back our Girls" campaign   143
British East India Company   101
Brown, Michael   113
Brown, Wendy   75, 86
Bush, George W.   139–40

Cáceres, Berta   87–90
Can Democracy Survive Global Capitalism? (Kuttner)   64

capitalism 6, 27
  democracy and 64
  elimination 156–7
  global 11–12
capitalist-desiring subjects 116
capitalist market 118–19
capitalist processes 4, 16, 20, 45, 69–70, 197 n.13
Casero-Ripollés, Andreu 143–4
Césaire, Aimé 44
Change the World without Taking Power (Holloway) 92
Chernow, Ron 77
citizenship 86–92
  for accountability democracy 91
  monitorial 84–5
  obligations 92
  public education and 88
  of representative democracy 90
  rights based 84–5
  skills 90
  world 89–90
Clean Clothes Campaign 167–8
climate crisis 12–13
  accountability for 174–80
  governments on 176–80
  society and 174–5
  solutions 176–7
  UNFCCC agreement for 177–80
Clinton, Bill 135–6
Cloward, Richard 146
colonialism 44–5
communication 61
Communist Manifesto (Marx and Engels) 70
community 42
Community Safety Act 171
consumer culture 117
counter-democracy 84–5
Counter-Democracy: Politics in an Age of Distrust (Rosanvallon) 84

counter-hegemonies 117
criminal guilt 52–3
Crouch, Collin 62–3, 91–2
Crucial Accountability (Patterson, Grenny, McMillan, Al Switzler, and Maxfield) 137
Cultivating Humanity: A Classical Defense of Reform in Liberal Education (Nussbaum) 89

Dakota Access Pipeline 178–80
de Beauvoir, Simone 55–6
democracy
  accountability 7–8, 10, 12, 18–20, 32, 80–5, 93, 129, 163–84
  building 163–84, 189–90
  citizenship for 91
  education for 88
  ethics of 35–58
  capitalism and 64
  in crisis 59–71
  direct 83
  domination, freedom from 65–71, 80
  electoral 13, 62–4, 84–6, 91
  illiberal 62, 64
  liberal 61–3
  monitory 83–5
  parliamentary 122–3
  representative 17–18, 83
  in societies 64–5
Democracy and Education (Dewey) 88
"Democracy in the Digital Communication Environment: A Typology" (Feenstra and Casero-Ripollés) 143–4
democratic traditions 76–7

deprivation 17
Dewey, John 88
dialogue 91
direct democracy 83
Discipline and Punish (Foucault) 116
Discourse on Colonialism (Césaire) 44
disruption sanction, for accountability 145–7
domination, freedom from 65–71

education 88
elections sanction, for accountability 147–8
electoral democracy 13, 62–4, 84–6, 91
End of Power: From Boardrooms to Battlefields and Churches to States: Why Being in Charge Isn't What It Used To Be, The (Naím) 65
Energy Transfer Partners 179
Enlightenment movement 43–5
"Enough of Deliberation: Politics is about Interests and Power," (Shapiro) 90
ethics 31
Ethics of Ambiguity, The (de Beauvoir) 55
Europe 63–4
European Union 63–4, 147
exploitation 114
externalities 155–6
Exxon-Mobil 99–100, 111, 130–1, 160
Eze, Michael Onyebuchi 42

feedback loops 28–9, 32
  for accountability 151–6
    action 152
    consequences 152

elements 152
evidence 152
market 153–6
pro-capitalist thought and 153–6
relevance 152
Feenstra, Ramón 143–4
Feinberg, Joel 149
Foucault, Michel 98–9, 106, 116
freedom 38–9, 78
  from domination 65–71, 80
  liberty as 77–8
free market 118, 120, 156, 161
Fromm, Eric 116

Galtung, Fredrik 124
Garner, Eric 9, 14, 96–7, 107, 112, 115, 171–2
Garzón, Baltazar 140
Gbadegesin, Segun 42
Getting Past Capitalism: History, Vision, Hope (Kaufman) 156
Glasberg, Davita Silfen 150
global capitalism 11–12
"Global Coalition against Corruption: Evaluating Transparency International, The" (Galtung and Pope) 124
globalization 64
Goetz, Thomas 152
Good Citizen, The (Schudson) 80
Gordon, Rebecca 139–40
governments 16–17, 45, 80, 92, 101, 160
  accountability 107–11, 130, 198 n.4
  on climate crisis 176–80
  democratic system of 107
  national 101, 110
  power in 12–13, 17, 92, 106–11
  racism in 19

Gramsci, Antonio 103, 117
Great Transformation, The
  (Polanyi) 119
Greece 67-8, 180-3
Greek economic crisis 11-12
Grounding for the Metaphysics of Morals (Kant) 42
guilt 35-6, 51-6
  criminal 52-3
  feelings of 51
  metaphysical 54-5
  moral 53-4
  political 53-4
  and responsibility, relationship between 50-1

Hall, Stuart 106
Hamilton, Alexander 77
Hamilton (Chernow) 77
"Harnessing the Power of Feedback Loops" (Goetz) 152
Harris, Cheryl 113-14
Hart, Jeffrey 101
History of Sexuality, The (Michel) 98-9
Holloway, John 92
homo oeconomicus 75, 80
homo politicus 75, 80, 86
humanity 17
human rights 149-51
Human Rights Enterprise, The (Armaline, Glasberg, and Purkayastha) 150
humility 55-6

illiberal democracy 62, 64
Imagined Communities: Reflections on the Origin and Spread of Nationalism (Anderson) 87
immigration 61-2

Imperative of Responsibility: In Search of an Ethics for the Technological Age, The (Jonas) 31
individuality 42
informed citizen 81
international law 139-41
International Monetary Fund 66, 70, 111

Jaspers, Karl 41, 52
Jefferson, Thomas 77-8
Jonas, Hans 31
Juliana vs. United States 139-41

Kant, Immanuel 42-4
Keane, John 82-3
King, Martin Luther, Jr. 97
Koterski, Joseph W. 41
Kuttner, Robert 62, 64

Lang, Anthony 57
legal sanctions, for accountability 139-41
liberal 76
  accountability 7
  democracy 61-2
  political theory 79
liberalism 63-4, 76-7, 79
liberties 38, 77-8
Life and Death of Democracy, The (Keane) 82
Locke, John 40, 75, 78, 119

Machiavelli 78
Malik, Charles 148
Manning, Chelsea 144
market 16, 161-2
  as autonomous and neutral 119
  capitalist 118-19
  feedback loop 153-6

free   118, 120, 156, 161
immunity   102–3
power of   102–3, 118–21
regulations   120
sanctions, for accountability   142–3
market-based social justice campaigns   142
Martin, Trayvon   113
Marx, Karl   6
Marxism   108–10
mass incarceration   14, 108, 136
Matthews, Jessica   100
Mazlumder, Turkish human rights organization   83
metaphysical guilt   54–5
money   193 n.2
monitory democracy   83–5
moral goodness   41
moral guilt   53–4
morality   3, 29–30, 32, 36, 41, 186, 189
  Kant's philosophy   42–4
  of power   49, 97–8
  and social connection   46–9
Mounk, Yascha   60–1
Movement for Black Lives   14–15, 113–18, 172–3
multi-media-saturated societies   83
Multipolar Globalization Emerging Economics and Development (Pieterse)   70

Naím, Moisés   65–6, 69
national sovereignty   63
nativist fears   62
nature, state of   37–9
Nazism   52–3
neofascism; *see* illiberal democracy
network of social relations   32, 45

Nixon, Richard   141
Nussbaum, Martha   89–90

Omi, Michael   104–5
oppression   6–7, 114

Panama Papers   144
Pantaleo, Daniel   9, 14, 96–7, 107, 112, 115, 171–2
parliamentary democracy   122–3
People vs. Democracy: Why Our Freedom Is in Danger and How to Save It, The (Mounk)   60
Personal Responsibility and Work Opportunity Act   135
Pettit, Philip   76, 78–9
Pieterse, Jan Nederveen   70
Pinochet, Augusto   140
Piven, Francis Fox   146
plunder   37
Poggi, Gianfranco   98
Polanyi, Karl   119
police violence   8–9, 14–15, 113, 133–4, 171–3
political accountability   103–4
political goodness   41
political guilt   53–4
politics   41, 74–81, 93
Politics (Aristotle)   75
polyarchy system   67
Poor People's Movements: Why They Succeed and How They Fail (Cloward and Piven)   146
Pope, Jeremy   124
Post-Democracy (Crouch)   91
Poulantzas, Nicos   109
poverty   129–30
power   97–104, 125
  to account   4–5, 121–5

accountability and   4–5, 7–8, 15, 19, 134–5
agency and   104–6
configurations of   4, 8–9, 103
   capitalist markets   8, 10–11
   governmental sovereignty   8, 12–13
   money   193 n.2
   systems of meaning   8, 14–15
   transnational processes   8, 11–12
destructive   95–125, 190
in governments   12–13, 17, 92, 101, 106–11
of market   102, 118–21
morality of   49, 97–8
nation-states   102
operations of   5, 7–9, 14, 18, 28, 100, 111–12
responsibility   48
social   98
state   6–7
in systems of meaning   112–18
Power of Market Fundamentalism: Karl Polanyi's Critique, The (Block and Sommers)   120
Prakash, Aseem   101
pro-capitalist thinking   6, 16–17, 19, 28–9
   accountability mechanisms and   32, 153–6
   expansion of   16
   social decisions   4
pro-capitalist thought   153–6
pseudo-accountability   5, 136–7
public education   88, 116
public-school systems   116
punishment   57
Purkayastha, Bandana   150

queer liberation movement   117
Question of German Guilt, The (Jaspers)   41, 52

racial formation   104–5
Racial Formation in the United States from the 1960s to the 1990s (Omi and Winant)   105
racism   19, 32, 51, 105, 115, 133
Rana, Sohel   10, 26, 29–30
Rana Plaza in Bangladesh (2013), collapse of   9–11, 24–8
   accountability for   29–33, 169–71
   capitalism and   27
   future prevention   167–71
   responsible for   26–7, 167–8
Reagan, Ronald   40
reforms   157
regulation sanctions, for accountability   141
representative democracy   17–18, 83
republican   76
republicanism   76–80
Republicanism: A Theory of Freedom in Government (Pettit)   76
Republic (Plato)   41
responsibilities   8, 18–19, 40–1, 56–8, 186–7, 189
   and accountability   8, 18–19, 132–4
   as collective ability   48–9
   and guilt, relationship between   50–1
   as interest   48, 167–8
   as power   48, 167–8
   as privilege   48, 167–8, 172, 179
   social connection model of   46–9
   without shame   50–1

"Responsibility and Global Justice: A Social Connection Model," (Young) 46
revolution 157–8
rights-bearing citizen 81–2
Rights Justice and the Bounds of Liberty (Feinberg) 149
rights sanction, for accountability 148–51
Robinson, William 66–7
Roe vs. Wade 150
Rosanvallon, Pierre 84–5
Russell, Bertrand 140

Sachs, Goldman 67
sanctions, for accountability mechanisms 8, 15, 18–20, 137–51, 194 n.6
  disruption 145–7
  elections 147–8
  legal 139–41
  market 142–3
  regulation 141
  rights 148–51
  scrutiny 143–5
Sartre, Jean-Paul 140
Schäuble, Wolfgang 67–8
Schedler, Andreas 103–4
Schudson, Michael 80–1
Schwarzenegger, Arnold 141
scrutiny sanctions, for accountability 143–5
Service Employees International Union (SEIU) 146
shame, responsibility without 50–1
Shapiro, Ian 90, 107
Silicon Valley 155
slavery 37, 44–5
Smith, Adam 16, 119
Snowden, Edward 144

social connections 40
  features of 47
  and morality 46–9
  responsibility and 46–9
social justice 97, 122, 142, 157, 182
social media 3, 60–1, 143, 179
social norm, violation of 57
social power 98
social processes, complexity of 2–3, 105–6, 114
social transformations 65
  as mentality 66
  as mobility 65–6
  as more 65
social welfare systems 5
societies 40–6
  accountability mechanisms 31
  building 41
  capitalist aspects of 4
  class 6
  climate crisis and 174–5
  democracies in 64–5
  multi-media-saturated 83
  pro-capitalist 16–19
Sommers, Margaret 120
State, Power, Socialism (Polantzas) 122

tax havens 112
Thatcher, Margaret 41
transnational corporations 4, 18, 100, 111–12, 123–5, 160, 188
Transpacific Partnership (TPP) 111–12
Transparency International (TI) 124–5
tribunals 140
Tsipras, Alexis 67–8
Two Treatises of Government (Locke) 40

undemocratic liberalism 63–4
Undoing the Demos: Neoliberalism's Stealth Revolution (Brown) 75
United Nations Declaration of Human Rights 148, 150
United Nations Framework Convention on Climate Change (UNFCCC) agreement 177–80
United States 61, 70, 108, 114–15, 117
  on climate change 9
  constitutional amendments 149–50
  electoral system in 81
  Juliana vs. United States case 139–41
  legalized abortion in 150
  police violence 14, 96–7, 107, 171–2
  Vietnam War and 140
  voting rights in 136
Universal Declaration of Human Rights 88

values, accountability 8, 14, 18, 115, 131–2
Varden, Helga 43
Vietnam War 140
violence 17; *see also* police violence
voice, accountability 8, 14, 18, 115, 135–7, 194 n.6

Walmart 155
watchdog function, scrutiny 144
Weheliye, Alexander 114
Where Do We Go from Here: Chaos or Community (King) 98
"White Man's Guilt" (Baldwin) 51
Williams, Patricia 113
Winant, Howard 104–5
World Bank 66, 70, 100
world citizenship 89–90
World Trade Organization 66, 111, 120, 160–1
Wynter, Sylvia 114

Young, Iris Marion 46–50, 56, 68, 133, 166, 168, 179, 183

Zakaria, Fareed 62